Shoulder Sleeve Insignia and Crest of the U. S. Army Vietnam

Dedicated to all Vietnam veterans and their families who supported them when they so unselfishly served their country in the United States Army.

E Book Edition ISBN - 978-1-884452-60-4
Softcover Edition ISBN - 978-1-884452-86-4

Copyright 2024 by MOA Press

All rights reserved. No part of this publication may be reproduced, stored in retrieval systems or transmitted by any means, electronic, mechanical or by photocopying, recording or by any information storage and retrieval system without permission from the publisher, except for the inclusion of brief quotations in a review.

Published by:

MOA Press (Medals of America Press)
114 Southchase Blvd. • Fountain Inn, SC 29644
www.moapress.com • www.usmedals.com

Shoulder Sleeve Insignia and Crest of the U. S. Army Vietnam

Table of Contents

Introduction	2
Army Shoulder Sleeve Insignia	4
Major headquarters In Vietnam	6
Divisions and Infantry Brigades in Vietnam	10
Commands and other Briadges	33

Introduction

The U.S. Army combat patches worn on the right shoulder of individual Vietnam veterans hold significant importance for several reasons:

Personal Achievement: Combat patches symbolize a soldier's direct participation in combat operations. They represent the individual's courage, dedication, and sacrifice in the service of their country. For Army Vietnam veterans, wearing a combat patch is a visible reminder of their personal experiences and contributions during wartime.

Unit Affiliation: Combat patches not only signify personal achievement but also indicate the unit the soldier served during combat. This affiliation with a specific unit fosters a sense of pride, camaraderie, and belonging among veterans. It serves as a visual link to the shared experiences and bonds forged during their war time service.

Recognition and Respect: Combat patches are widely recognized within the military community and by civilians as symbols of honor and valor. They carry with them the respect and admiration of others who understand the challenges and sacrifices associated with combat service. For veterans, wearing a combat patch is a way to be recognized and respected for their service and sacrifices.

Legacy and Tradition: Combat patches often have a rich history and tradition associated with the units they represent. Veterans who wear these patches not only honor their own service but also pay tribute to the legacy of the unit and the soldiers who came before them. This connection to tradition is deeply meaningful to Vietnam veterans, providing a sense of continuity and belonging to United States military heritage.

Remembrance and Reflection: For many veterans, wearing a combat patch serves as a reminder of their wartime experiences and the comrades they served alongside, including those who made the ultimate sacrifice. It can evoke a range of emotions,of both pride and camaraderie from their time in combat.

Overall, the U.S. Army combat patches worn on the right shoulder hold profound significance for individual veterans, representing personal achievement, unit affiliation, recognition, respect, tradition, remembrance, and reflection. They serve as enduring symbols of honor and valor, connecting veterans to their military service and the shared bonds of those who have served in combat.

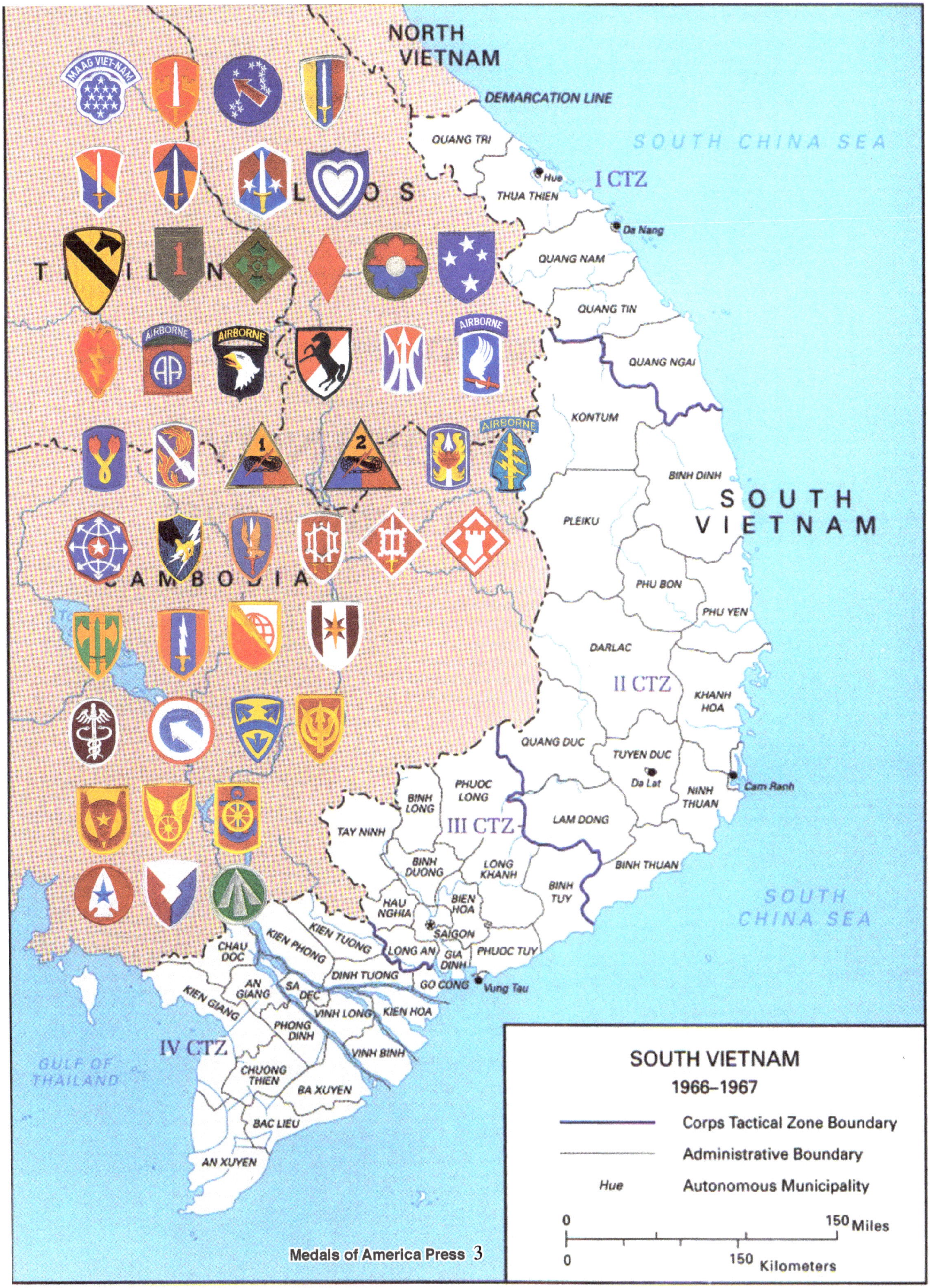
NORTH VIETNAM
DEMARCATION LINE
SOUTH CHINA SEA
LAOS
THAILAND
CAMBODIA
SOUTH VIETNAM
MAAG VIET-NAM
AIRBORNE
AA
AIRBORNE
AIRBORNE
AIRBORNE
1
2
1
I CTZ
II CTZ
III CTZ
IV CTZ
QUANG TRI
Hue
THUA THIEN
Da Nang
QUANG NAM
QUANG TIN
QUANG NGAI
KONTUM
BINH DINH
PLEIKU
PHU BON
PHU YEN
DARLAC
KHANH HOA
QUANG DUC
TUYEN DUC
Da Lat
Cam Ranh
NINH THUAN
PHUOC LONG
BINH LONG
TAY NINH
LAM DONG
BINH THUAN
BINH DUONG
LONG KHANH
BINH TUY
HAU NGHIA
BIEN HOA
SAIGON
KIEN TUONG
LONG AN
GIA DINH
PHUOC TUY
Vung Tau
CHAU DOC
KIEN PHONG
DINH TUONG
GO CONG
AN GIANG
SA DEC
KIEN GIANG
VINH LONG
KIEN HOA
PHONG DINH
VINH BINH
CHUONG THIEN
BA XUYEN
BAC LIEU
AN XUYEN
GULF OF THAILAND
SOUTH CHINA SEA
SOUTH VIETNAM
1966–1967
Corps Tactical Zone Boundary
Administrative Boundary
Hue
Autonomous Municipality
0
150 Miles
0
150 Kilometers

Army Shoulder Sleeve Insignia and Unit Crest

Since ancient times, the identification of friend or foe has been a battlefield problem. Roman armies often would have the various units wear different colored horse hair in their helmets to provide commanders a quick overall view of their troops disposition. In the Middle Ages, knights would have their family's coat-of-arms painted on their shields or on a banner providing the troops an emblem as a central point to rally around during combat.

During the nineteenth century, the newly formed United States had no real need for battlefield identification until the Civil War *(1861-1865)*. With the massive build-up of armies and the tactics of the time exacerbating the problem, the Union army attempted to resolve the need by assigning each army corps an emblem to be sewn to the tops of caps to provide officers on horseback the ability to identify their respective troops. These emblems were common geometric designs: circle, square, triangle, etc. for the corps. Each division of the corps used the same emblem but in a different color. After the end of hostilities, and the reduction of forces, the custom died out until the last months of World War I.

The rebirth of this concept in the twentieth century was not without controversy. The story is told that when the 81st Infantry Division disembarked in France in 1918, the members of the division were all wearing a *"patch"* on their left shoulder depicting a black bobcat on an olive-drab background. This was to recall that they had trained on the banks of Bobcat Creek at Camp Jackson, SC. When word of this event reached higher headquarters, there being no regulations to cover this activity, orders were immediately issued to have the offending emblem removed.

The Commanding General of the 81st Division made a personal appeal to General Pershing to permit his troops to continue wearing the patch. General Pershing is reported to have said: "Go ahead. But, be sure that you are worthy of it". General Pershing then not only rescinded the order but, realizing the morale value of this simple piece of cloth, ordered that all other units of the American Expeditionary Force would immediately create similar designs for their troops to wear. It was felt that this would have a positive morale effect on the troops in the trenches and give the members a sense of comradeship and unit cohesion that was necessary for that type of warfare. It permitted the individual to feel that he was a member of a particular group and could take pride in being associated with the accomplishments of that unit. This opened the gates of creativity and soon the Army had designs on everything - uniforms, vehicles, equipment and buildings.

During the Vietnam War the shoulder sleeve insignia *(SSI)* was an embroidered patch worn on the shoulders of Army uniforms to identify the primary headquarters a Soldier was assigned. Most units smaller than brigades did not have SSI, but wore the SSI of a higher headquarters. The Army is unique among the Armed Forces in that all soldiers are required to wear the designated unit patch of their headquarters as part of their military uniforms.

Shoulder sleeve insignia receive their name from the fact that they are most commonly worn on the upper left sleeve of the field uniform and Army Green uniform. However, they can be placed on other locations, notably on the side of a helmet. Shoulder sleeve insignia worn on the upper right sleeve of Army uniforms denote former wartime service.

During the Vietnam War soldiers wearing the kakai uniform wore their unit patch suspended by a hanger below their breast pocket as shown below.

Shoulder Sleeve Insignia and Crest of the U.S. Army Vietnam

U.S. Army Vietnam Major Unit Shoulder Sleeve Insignia and Unit Crest

Subdued patches and insignia were introduced during the Vietnam War and were made mandatory for wear on the field uniform starting 1 July, 1970. SSIs are generally authorized only for units commanded by a general officer. In the early 1960s, separate armor regiments began creating SSI, and the number of separate brigades increased. Today, most separate brigades have their own SSI, but those brigades permanently assigned to divisions do not.

VICTORY
STEADFAST AND LOYAL
RENDEZVOUS WITH DESTINY

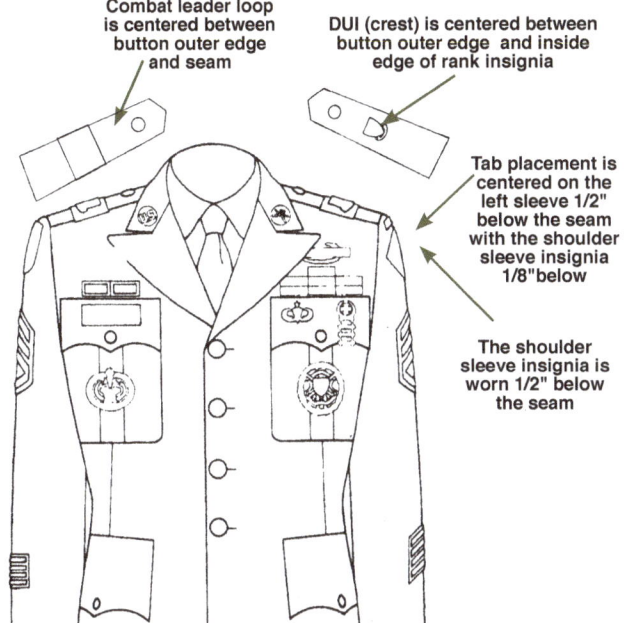

The other unique unit identification insignia for Army units in Vietnam was their unit crest officially called a distinctive unit insignia or DUI. These are a metallic heraldic badge or device which is derived from the coat of arms authorized a major unit or regiment. The U.S. Army Institute of Heraldry is responsible for the design, development and authorization of all DUIs.

Up until 1965, only regiments and separate battalions were authorized a coat of arms and distinctive units insignia. During the Vietnam War major commands, field hospitals, corps, logistics commands and certain other units – Field Forces for example were authorized distinctive unit insignia. Soldiers wore their unit crest on the shoulder loops of the enlisted green jacket and kaiki shirt centered on the shoulder loops an equal distance from the outside shoulder seam to the outside edge of the button, with the base of the insignia toward the outside shoulder seam. Officers and Warrant officers also wore it in the same position, however enlisted personnel also wore their unit crest on the front edge of their folding garrison hat.

When a Unit's Crest is designed by the Institute of Heraldry, a careful study is made of the history and battle honors of the unit. The most important decorations, honors, combat service and missions are represented in the design of the insignia. Sometimes two centuries of history are condensed into symbolism for one distinctive unit insignia.

VOLENS ET POTENS

7th Inf. Regt.

Combat leader loop is centered between button outer edge and seam
DUI (crest) is centered between button outer edge and inside edge of rank insignia
Tab placement is centered on the left sleeve 1/2" below the seam with the shoulder sleeve insignia 1/8"below
The shoulder sleeve insignia is worn 1/2" below the seam

Units Created in/for Vietnam

Many of the units that served in Vietnam were created specifically for the war and disbanded after serving under multiple branches. The creation of units and divisions sprung from the increasing need of U.S. forces in South Vietnam as the conflict raged on.

Some of the major units that were created and disbanded after Vietnam are:

MACV, Military Assistance Command

United States Army Vietnam

I Field Force, Vietnam

II Field Force, Vietnam

1st Aviation Brigade

MAC-V SOG

MAC SOG

✪ Military Assistant Advisory Group Vietnam, MAAG-V

Entered RVN: 1950
Withdrew from RVN: 1965
Locale: Saigon

In September 1950, US President Harry Truman sent the Military Assistance Advisory Group *(MAAG)* to Vietnam to assist the French in the First Indochina War. The MAAG Vietnam patch was worn by personnel assigned to the Army mission : Military Assistance Advisory Group, Vietnam which replaced MAAG-Indochina, MAAG Vietnam arrived in Vietnam on 1 November 1955 and departed on 15 May 1964. During this group's service, military advisor strength was increased from 746 in 1961 to over 3,400 at the beginning of 1963. They were replaced in 1962 by United States Military Assistance Command, Vietnam *(MACV)*.

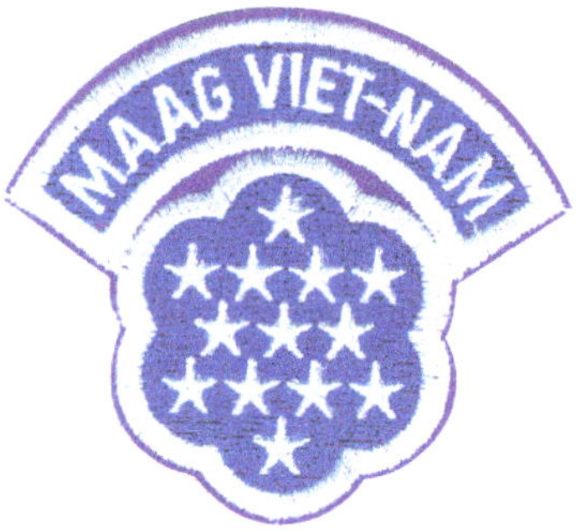
MAAG VIET-NAM

Worn from: April 1956 - March 1965.
Approved for local wear only.
No Distinctive Unit Insignia

✪ US Military Assistance Command Vietnam, MAC-V

Entered RVN: 1962
Withdrew from RVN: 1973
Locale: Saigon

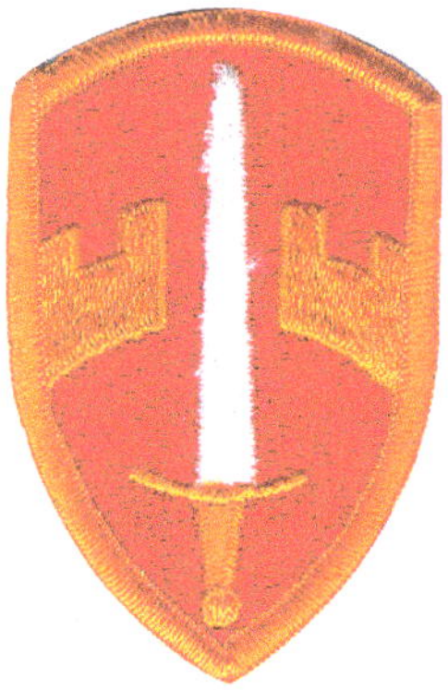

No Distinctive Unit Insignia

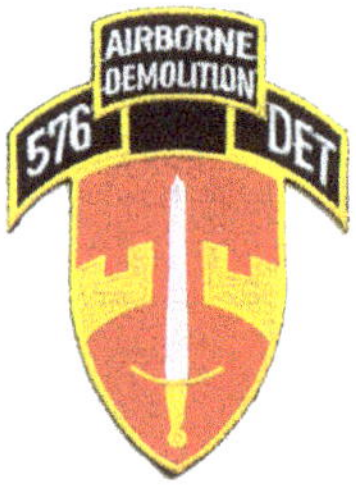
AIRBORNE
DEMOLITION
576
DET

576th Abn. Demo. Det.

Shoulder Sleeve Insignia

On a red shield 3 inches in height and 2 inches in width overall, between two segments of a yellow arched embattled fess, a sword, with yellow hilt and white blade, point to top, all within $^1/_8$ inch yellow border.

Yellow and red are the Vietnam colors. The red ground alludes to the infiltration and aggression from beyond the embattled "wall" *(i.e., the Great Wall of China)*. The opening in the *"wall"* through which this infiltration and aggression flow is blocked by the sword representing United States military aid and support. The *"wall"* is arched and the sword pointed upward in reference to the offensive action pushing the aggressors back.

The shoulder sleeve insignia was originally approved for the U.S. Army personnel serving in Vietnam on 10 February 1966. It was amended to correct the authorization to wear by U.S. Army personnel assigned to the U.S. Military Assistance Command, Vietnam, retroactive to 10 February 1966 on 22 September 1971.

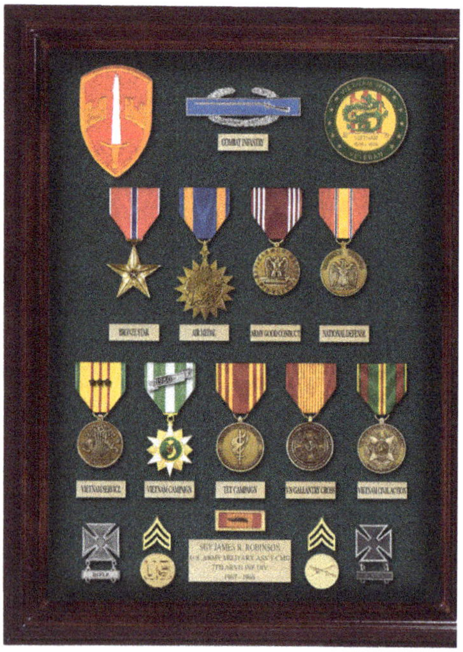

United States Army Pacific, USARPAC

Shoulder Sleeve Insignia

On a blue disc 2 3/4 inches in diameter, a red arrow fimbriated white, pointing upward bendwise at a 30 degree angle between the star polaris, the seven stars of Ursa Major, and the four stars of the Southern Cross, all white.

The arrow is representative of the strength and valor of the Armed Forces of the United States while the location of the Pacific Ocean Areas is indicated by Polaris, the seven star of Ursa Major, and the constellation of the Southern Cross.

The insignia was originally approved for the United States Army Forces, Pacific Ocean Areas on 18 Oct 1944; redesignated for United States Army Forces Middle Pacific on 8 Sep 1945; redesignated for United States Army Forces, Pacific Ocean Areas on 1 Nov 1945; redesignated for United States Army Pacific on 4 Dec 1947; redesignated United States Army Western Command effective 23 Mar 1979; and redesignated for the United States Army, Pacific effective 22 Aug 1990.

Its insignia, designed in 1944, depicted the axis of advance across the Central Pacific.

Distinctive Unit Insignia

Distinctive Unit Insignia

A silver color metal and enamel device 1 3/16 inches in height overall, consisting of a disc dived horizontally with six wavy alternating blue and silver bars, surmounted diagonally by a stylized red arrow, point up, bearing a silver diamond, and along the edge of the disc below the arrow and from base to tip of the arrow, a silver palm frond.

Red, white and blue are used to refer to both our national colors and the organization's shoulder sleeve insignia. The disc with its wavy blue and silver *(white)* bars is symbolic of water and represents the Pacific and its divisions of land and sea areas with which the United States Army Pacific is concerned. The arrow of war, suggested by the unit's shoulder sleeve insignia, relates to the overall mission. The diamond on the arrowhead alludes to *"Diamond Head"* and refers to the island of Oahu, Hawaii, the unit's home site. The palm denotes merit and leadership and also refers to the foliage of the Pacific areas.

The distinctive unit insignia was originally approved for US Army Pacific on 26 Feb 1969; rescinded on 20 Jan 1975; reinstated and authorized for US Army Western Command effective 23 Mar 1979; and redesignated for US Army Pacific effective 22 Aug 1990.

United States Army Vietnam, USARV

Shoulder Sleeve Insignia

The United States Army Vietnam patch has a white sword with a gold hilt in the center of the patch that is the same shape as the MACV patch. This patch features one gold, one blue, and one red horizontal stripe in the patch with a white border. Blue represents the United states and red and yellow represent Vietnam. Together with the sword this patch represented United States military aid and support.

US Army: Vietnam
Landed in Vietnam: 20 July 1965
Left South Vietnam: 15 May 1972
Locale: Long Binh

No Distinctive Unit Insignia

United States Army, Vietnam (USARV) was a corps-level support command of the United States Army in the Vietnam War. USARV was created on 20 July 1965 out of the U.S. Army Support Command, Vietnam.

I Field Force, Vietnam

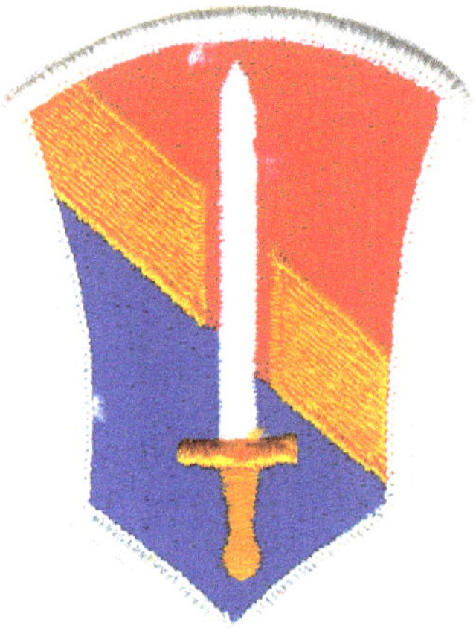

Landed in RVN: 15 March 1966
Left RVN: 30 April 1971
Locale: Nha Trang

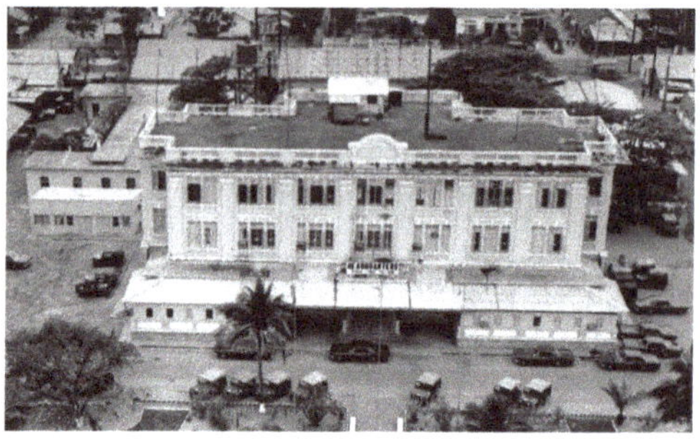

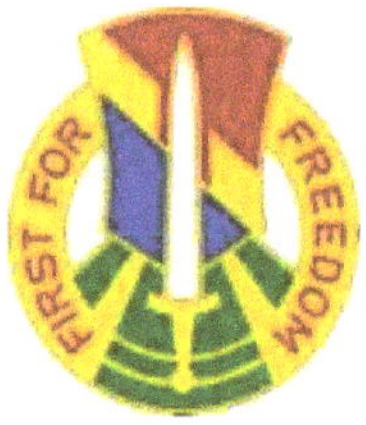
FIRST FOR FREEDOM

Distinctive Unit Insignia

Shoulder Sleeve Insignia

The crusader's sword *(the "Sword of Freedom")* was suggested by the shoulder sleeve insignia previously authorized for the United States Military Assistance Command, Vietnam, and the United States Army, Vietnam. The one diagonal refers to the numerical designation of the I Field Force. The sword "piercing" the red area alludes to the constant probing of enemy territory and positions and the driving back and crushing of enemy forces. The colors red, white and blue are the national colors of the United States, and the colors yellow and red, are those of Vietnam. The colors blue, red and yellow are also those of the three major combat arms: Infantry, Artillery and Armor. The silhouette of the shield is shaped like a battle-ax to symbolize the smashing power of the I Field Force and the constant combat readiness of its personnel to engage the enemy. The battle-ax shape, in itself, is also an additional I Field Force identification. The shoulder sleeve insignia was approved on 5 October 1966.

Distinctive Unit Insignia

The red, gold (yellow) and blue device is in the shape of the authorized shoulder sleeve insignia of the I Field Force, Vietnam, the crusader sword represents the numerical "One *(of "First")*. The green mountain reflect the Central Highlands, the open circular scroll simulates an envelopment of movement. The motto "First For Freedom" reflects the organization's spirit and determination.

II Field Force, Vietnam

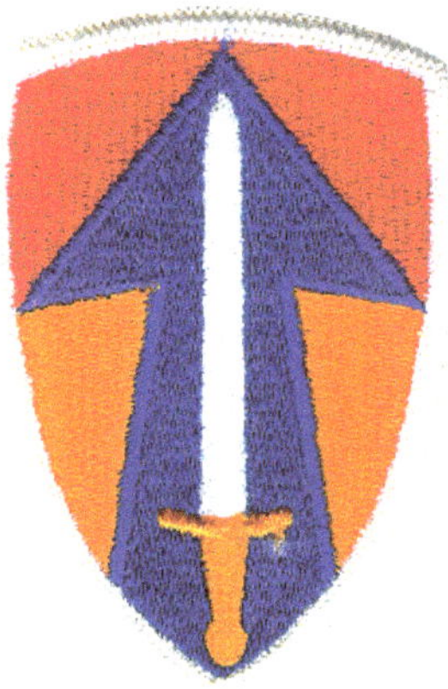

Landed in RVN: 15 March 1966
Left RVN: 2 May 1971
Locale: Bein Hoa, Long Binh

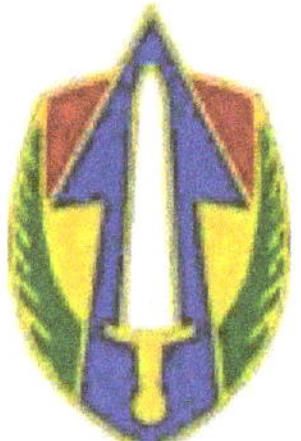

Distinctive Unit Insignia

Shoulder Sleeve Insignia

The shape of the shield and the unsheathed crusader's sword *(the "Sword of Freedom")* were suggested by the shoulder sleeve insignia previously authorized for the United States Military Assistance Command, Vietnam, and the United States Army, Vietnam.

The stylized blue arrow and sword are used to represent the purpose and military might of the II Field Force pressing against, sweeping back, and breaking through enemy forces symbolized by the red areas.

The dividing of the red and yellow areas of the shield into two parts allude to the numerical designation of the II Field Force, the colors red and yellow also being those of Vietnam. The colors red, white and blue are the national colors of the United States and further allude to the three major combat arms: Infantry, Artillery and Armor.

Distincitive Unit Insignia

The operations and numerical designation are indicated by the scarlet and gold *(yellow)* device in the shape and background design of the authorized shoulder sleeve insignia of the II Field Force, Vietnam, and by the unsheathed Crusader sword which has become associated with Vietnam and the blue stylized arrow both of which were also suggested by the shoulder sleeve insignia and when taken together allude to the numeral II *(or Second)*. The scarlet and gold *(yellow)* background and green palm fronds refer to the major combat operational area of the II Field Force which includes the defense of Saigon. The palm fronds are also symbolic of successful achievement

Capital Military Assistance Command

Landed in RVN: 4 June 1968
Left RVN: 19 March 1973
Locale: Saigon

No Distinctive Unit Insignia

Shoulder Sleeve Insignia

On a hexagon 2 $^{1}/_{4}$ inches in width and 3 inches in height, the vertical sides 1 $^{13}/_{16}$ inches in length, divided saltirewise into two unequal ultramarine blue areas and two equal scarlet areas, the saltire division lines issuing from the two lower corresponding angles of the hexagon and intersecting $^{7}/_{8}$ inch from the upper angle, a vertical unsheathed crusader's sword, point up, with white blade and yellow hilt, between in base two white five-pointed stars of a size inscribed in a circle $^{5}/_{8}$ inch one point up, the vertical axis of each star coinciding with the saltire division lines and the center of each star $^{13}/_{16}$ inch from the two lower corresponding angles all within a $^{1}/_{8}$ inch white border.

Symbolism

The crusader's sword point up, with white blade and yellow hilt appears on both the shoulder sleeve insignia of the United States Army Vietnam *(on an ultramarine blue base)* and of the United States Military Assistance Command Vietnam *(on a scarlet base)*. The sword, a symbol of strength and courage, refers in this instance to the Capital Military Assistance Command and with the ultramarine blue and scarlet base provides the link with USARV and USMACV as the superior headquarters.

The white five-pointed star is a United States symbol and is also similar to that of the Army of the Republic of Vietnam; the two stars placed on either side of the guard of the unsheathed sword refer to the constant and combined efforts of the United States and the Army of the Republic of Vietnam in protecting Saigon, the capital of South Vietnam. The scarlet color also represents the Artillery which provides surveillance and counter measures against enemy rockets and mortar attacks, the blue color referring to the Infantry which continually patrols in and near Saigon to prevent enemy infiltration and ground attack. The shoulder sleeve insignia was approved on 29 July 1969. It was cancelled effective 1 April 1970.

XXIV Corps "Honed in Combat"

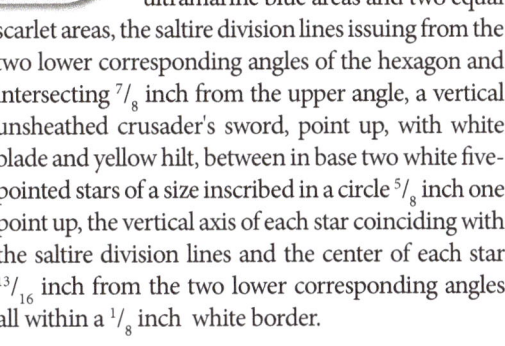

Shoulder Sleeve Insignia

On a blue shield 2 $^{7}/_{8}$ inches in height and 2 $^{1}/_{2}$ inches in width a white heart, a blue heart and a white heart superimposed one upon the other. It is an arbitrary design and is in the colors of the corps.

Landed in RVN: 15 Aug 1968
Left RVN: 30 June 1972
Locale: Phu Bai, Da Nang

HONED IN COMBAT

Distinctive Unit Insignia

Distinctive Unit Insignia

A gold color metal and enamel device 1 $^{3}/_{16}$ inches in height overall consisting of a gold disc within an annulet divided horizontally the upper half of white and the lower half of blue and bearing a blue heart *(of the same shape as that on the authorized shoulder sleeve insignia of the XXIV Corps)*. The "Auricles" and the tip touching the inner periphery of the annulet surmounted saltirewise by an unsheathed crusader's sword point up, blade of white and hilt gold, and a red stylized arrow, point up, within the blue heart, above a concentric gold scroll lined with red and bearing the inscription *"Honed In Combat"* in red letters.

The design is based on the authorized shoulder sleeve insignia of the XXIV Corps. The gold disc, symbolic of the sun, alludes to the Pacific Islands which the XXIV Corps is associated. The encircling white and blue annulet refers to the white beaches and blue water of the Pacific: Hawaii *(the annulet also simulating the letter "O" for Oahu where the Corps was initially activated 8 April 1944)* and the Philippines and Ryukyus campaigns the Corps participated in World War II. The red arrow refers to assault landing at Leyte and the blue, white and red colors of the insignia refer to the Philippine Presidential Unit Citation awarded the Corps for the period of 17 October 1944 to 4 July 1945. The Crusader's sword is for service in Vietnam where the Corps was activated 15 August 1968 as the successor to the Provisional Corps, Vietnam. In allusion to the motto *"Honed in Combat"* the red stylized arrow may be likened to the "whetstone of combat" on which the sword has been and is being honed.

1st Cavalry Division "First Team"

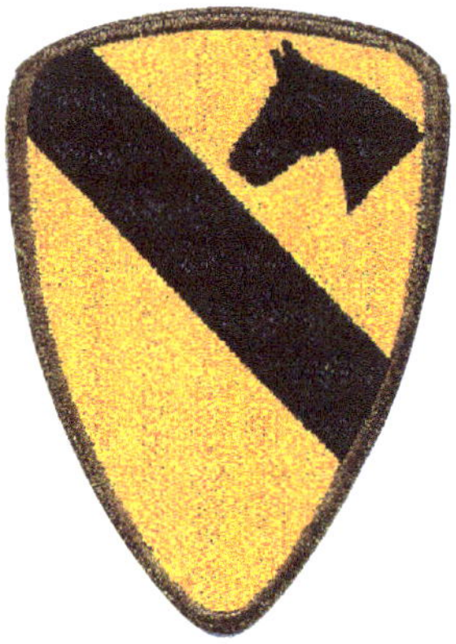

Shoulder Sleeve Insignia

On a yellow triangular Norman shield with rounded corners 5 $^{1}/_{4}$ inches in height overall, a black diagonal stripe extending over the shield from upper left to lower right and in the upper right a black horse's head cut off diagonally at the neck all within a $^{1}/_{8}$ inch green border.

The color yellow, the traditional Cavalry color, and the horse's head refer to the Division's original Cavalry structure. Black, symbolic of iron, alludes to the transition to tanks and armor. The black diagonal stripe represents a sword baldric and is a mark of military honor; it also implies movement *"up the field"* and thus symbolizes aggressive élan and attack. The one diagonal bend, as well as the one horse's head, also alludes to the Division's numerical designation.

The shoulder sleeve insignia was originally approved for the 1st Cavalry Division on 3 January 1921, with several variations in colors of the bend and horse's head to reflect the subordinate elements of the division. The current design was authorized for wear by all subordinate elements of the Division on 11 December 1934, and previous authorization for the variations was cancelled. The insignia was redesignated for the 1st Air Cavalry Division on 5 August 1968. It was redesignated for 1st Cavalry Division *(Airmobile)* on 10 September 1968. The insignia was redesignated for the 1st Cavalry Division on 24 May 1971.

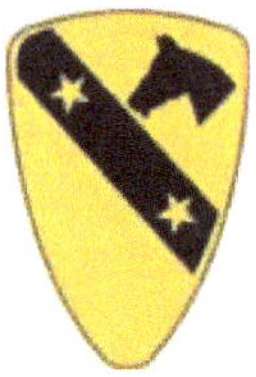

Distinctive Unit Insignia

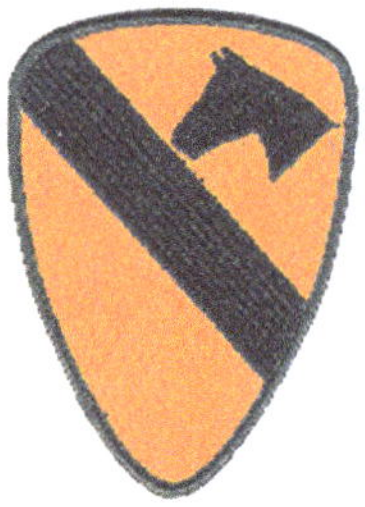

1St Cav. Div. Od Border

Landed in RVN:11 Sept. 1965
Left RVN: 29 April 1971
Locale: Pleiku, Binh Dinh, Quang Tri,

Distinctive Unit Insignia

A metal and enameled device 1 inch in height overall consisting of a gold colored Norman shield with a black horse's head couped in sinister chief, and a black bend charged with two five-pointed stars.

The device is a miniature reproduction of the 1st Cavalry Division's shoulder sleeve insignia with the addition of two five-pointed stars. The Division Commander and the Division Staff wore the distinctive insignia design from 1922 to 1934 as a shoulder sleeve insignia.

The distinctive unit insignia was originally approved for the 1st Cavalry Division on 25 August 1965. It was redesignated for the 1st Air Cavalry Division on 5 August 1968. It was redesignated for the 1st Cavalry Division *(Airmobile)* on 10 September 1968. The insignia was redesignated for the 1st Cavalry Division on 24 May 1971.

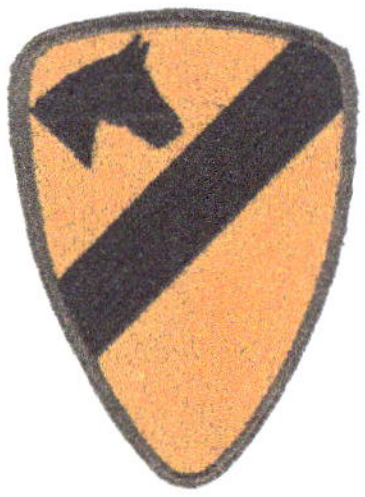

1st Cav. Div Combat Veteran.

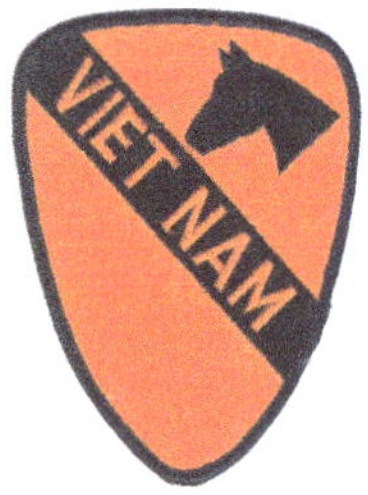
VIET NAM

Vietnam

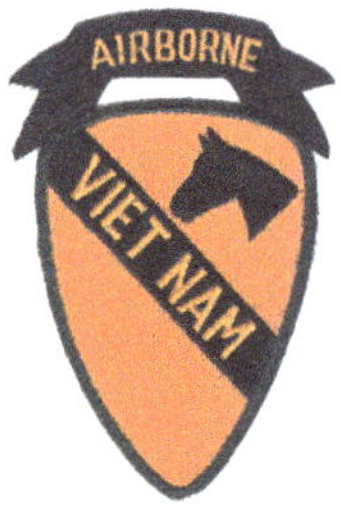
AIRBORNE
VIET NAM

Airborne Vietnam

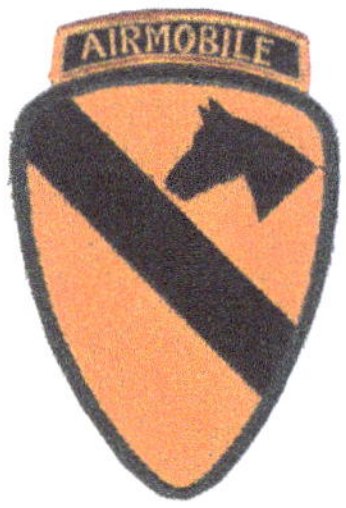
AIRMOBILE

Airmobile

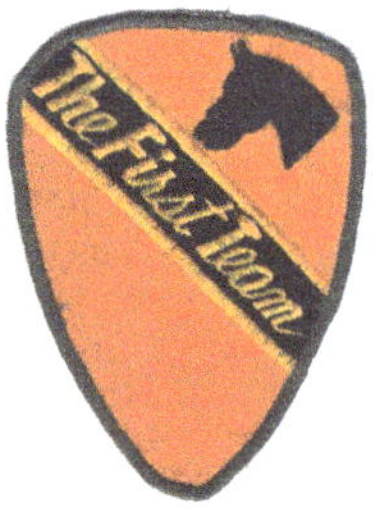
The First Team

The First Team

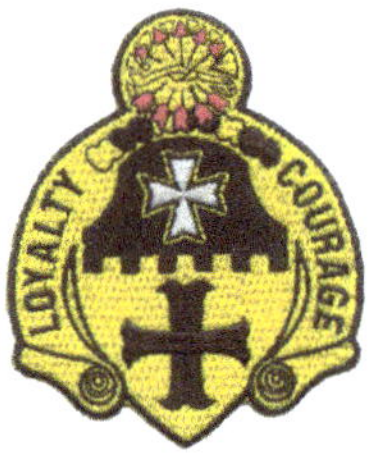
LOYALTY
COURAGE

1st & 2nd Bn.
5th Cav. Regt.

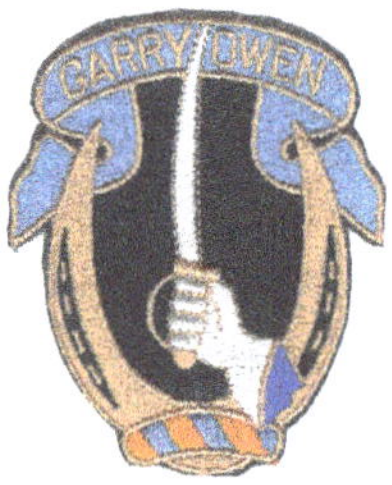
GARRY OWEN

1st , 2nd & 5th Bn.
7th Cav. Regt.

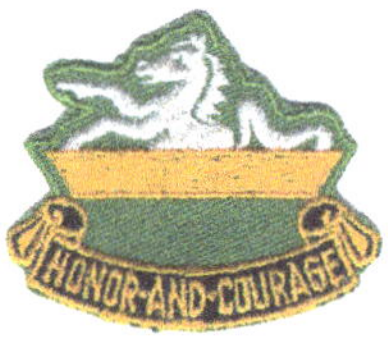
HONOR AND COURAGE

1st & 2nd Bn.
8th Cav. Regt.

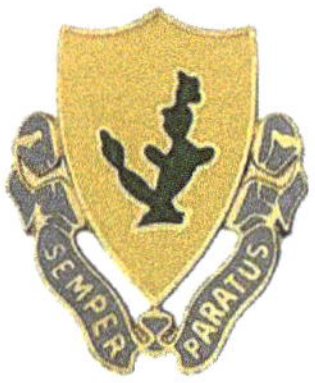
SEMPER
PARATUS

1st & 2nd Bn.
12th Cav. Regt.

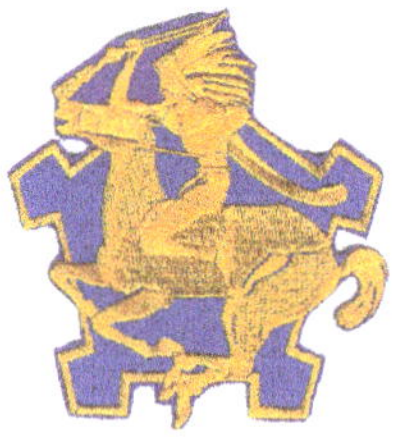

1st Sqn.
9th Cav. Regt.

1st Cav Division "Artillery"

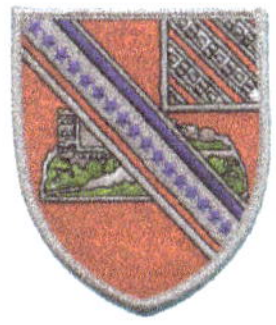

2/17th
FA Regt.

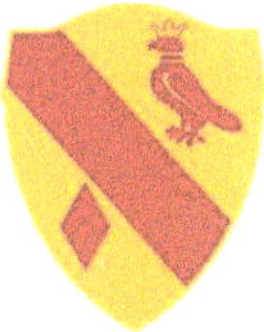

2/19th
FA Regt.

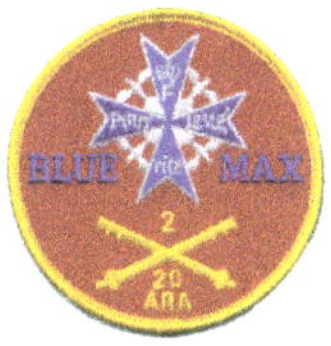
BLUE MAX

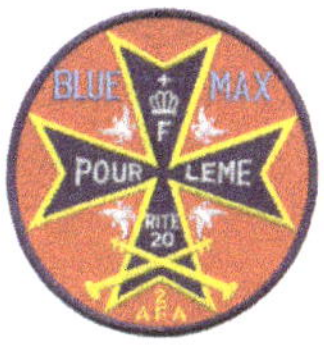
BLUE MAX
POUR LEME

2/20th
FA Regt.

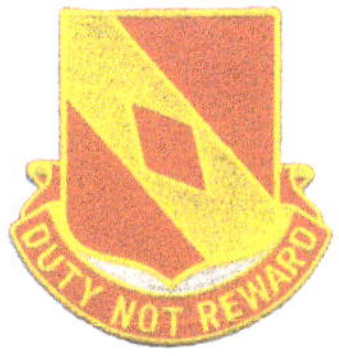
DUTY NOT REWARD

2/20th
FA Regt.

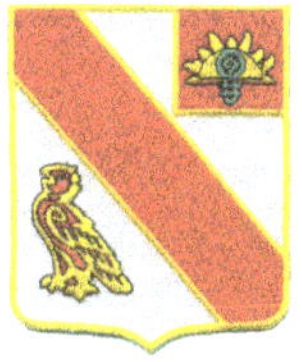

1/21th
FA Regt.

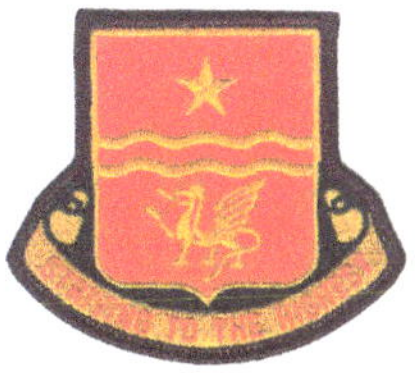

1/30th
FA Regt.

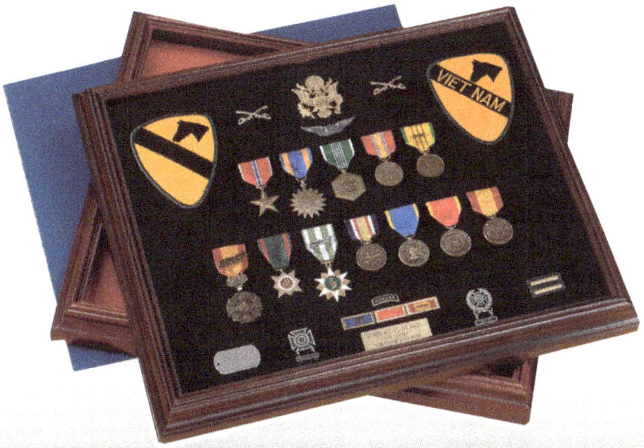
VIET NAM

1st Cav Division Aviation

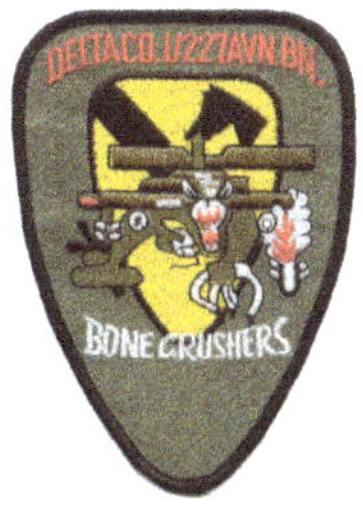
BONE CRUSHERS

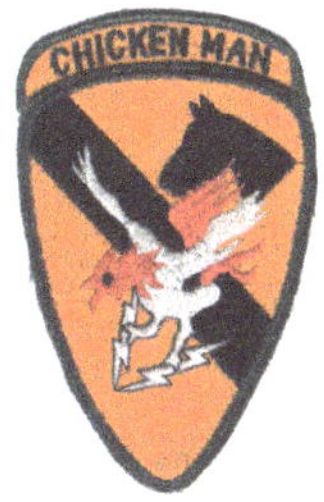
CHICKEN MAN

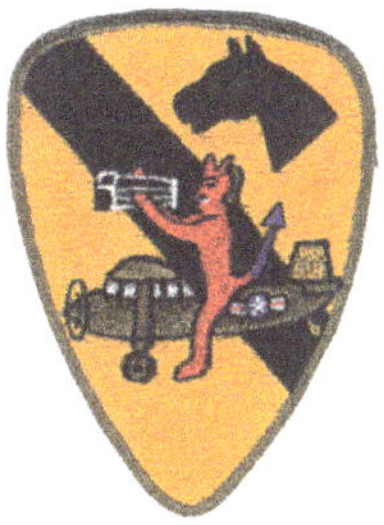

1st Cav Division Cav

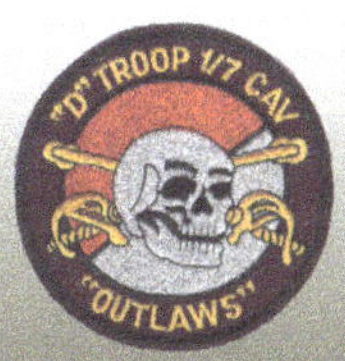
"D" TROOP 1/7 CAV
"OUTLAWS"

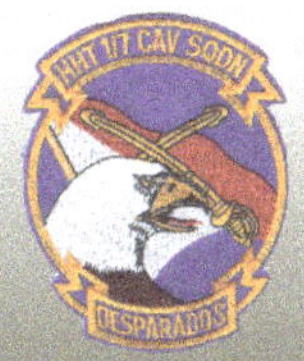
DESPARADOS

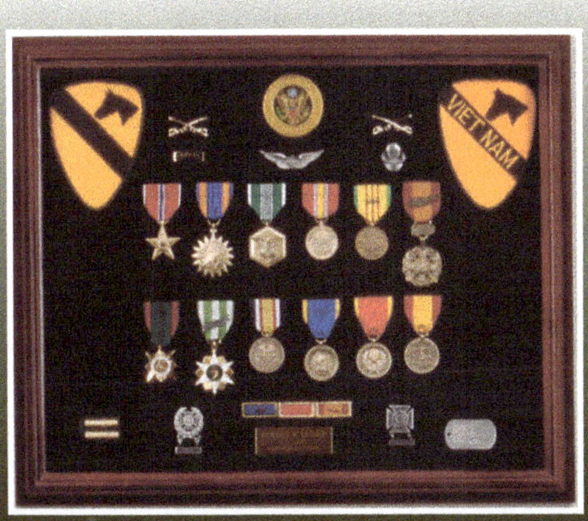
VIET NAM

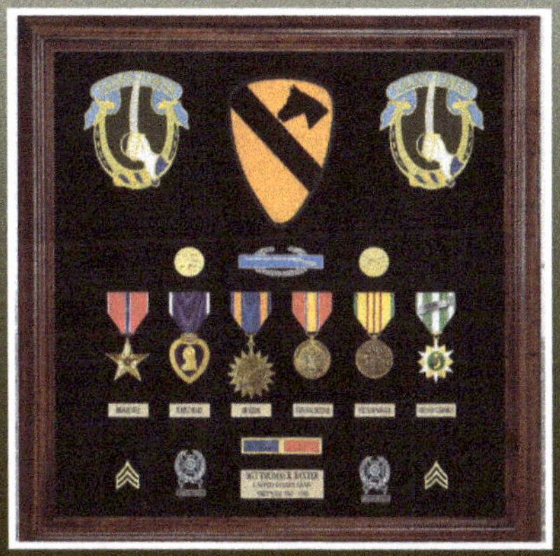

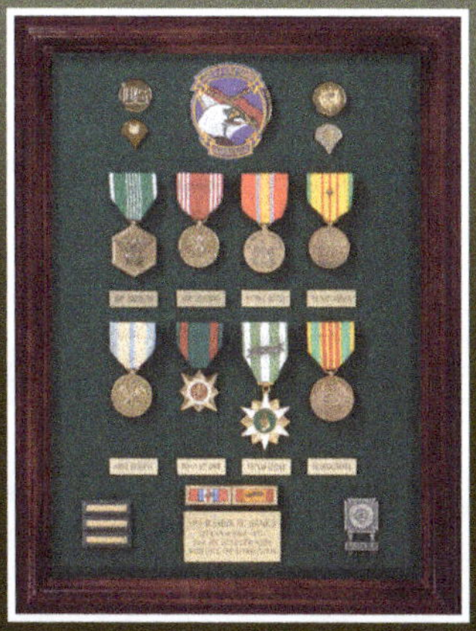

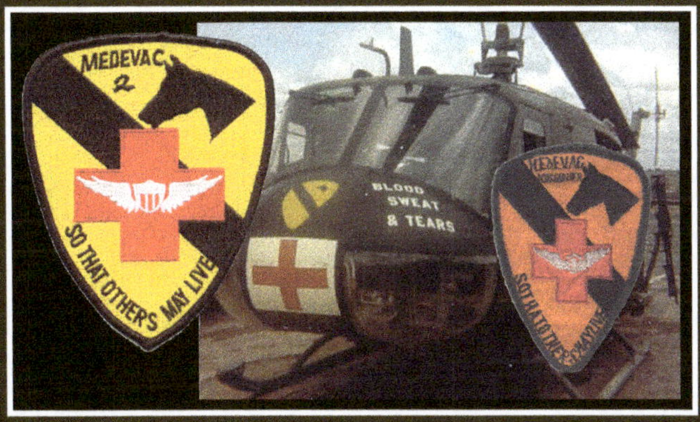
MEDEVAC
2
SO THAT OTHERS MAY LIVE
BLOOD
SWEAT
& TEARS

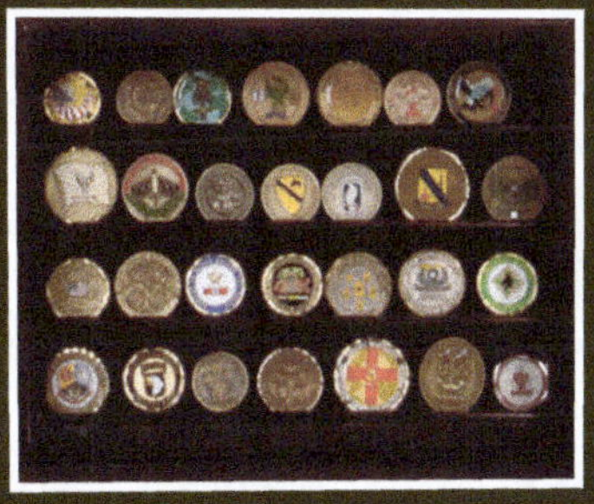

1st Infantry Division "Big Red One"

Shoulder Sleeve Insignia

On an olive drab shield 2 $\frac{1}{2}$ inches (in width and 3 $\frac{3}{4}$ inches in height overall (the parallel sides 2 $\frac{1}{2}$ inches in length with a 90 degree angle pointed base) a red Arabic numeral "1" *(1 $\frac{3}{4}$ inches in height overall).*

Landed in RVN: 2 Oct. 1965
Left RVN: 15 April 1970
Locale: Binh Long, Lai Khe

The numeral identifies the Division's designation. The shoulder sleeve insignia was originally approved for the 1st Division on 31 October 1918, as a red number "1" and amended on 31 March 1927, to include the background of the insignia in the design. It was redesignated for the 1st Infantry Division on 19 August 1942. The insignia was amended to revise the description on 6 October 1972.

Distinctive Unit Insignia

Distinctive Unit Insignia

An oval-shaped gold color metal and enamel device 1 $\frac{1}{8}$ inches *(2.86 cm)* in height overall consisting of a gold color metal background encircled by an elliptical band divided horizontally of red to the top and blue to base, inscribed on the blue the motto "VICTORY" in gold color metal letters; centered on the device is the figure from the 1st Division monument, modeled, in gold color metal, with wings and upraised arms extending over the red portion of the band.

Symbolism

The colors red and blue are from the distinguishing flags of Infantry Divisions. The figure portion is that of the 1st Infantry Division Monument, located in Washington, DC.

The distinctive unit insignia was originally approved for Headquarters, Headquarters Detachment and Headquarters, Special Troops, 1st Division on 9 December 1930. It was redesignated for wear by all non-color-bearing elements of the 1st Infantry Division on 2 September 1965. The insignia was amended to revise the description and add a symbolism on 14 January 1974.

First Infantry Division Assigned Infantry Battalions

| 1St & 2Nd Bn 2Nd Inf. Regt. | 1St & 2Nd Bn 16Th Inf. Regt. | 1St & 2D Bn 18Th Inf. Regt. | 1St Bn 26Th Inf. Regt. | 1St Bn 28Th Inf. Regt. |

First Infantry Division Assigned Artillery Battalions

| 1St Bn 5Th Artillery Regt. | 8Th Bn 6Th Artillery Regt. | 1st Bn 7Th Fld. Artillery Regt. | 6St Bn 15Th Artillery Regt. | 2Nd Bn 33Rd Fld. Artillery Regt. |

Shoulder Sleeve Insignia and Crest of the U.S. Army Vietnam

Evolution of the 1st Infantry Division Patch WW 1 to Today

First Infantry Division Aviation

1st Avn. Regt. 2nd Battalion | 1st Inf. Div. Avn. Sect. | 1st Inf. Div. 1st Avn Regt. | 1st Inf. Div. Avn. Regt. | 162nd Avn. Co.

First Infantry Division Support

16th A.C.R. C Troop | 1st Sqn. 4th Cav. Regt. | 1st Engr. Bn. | 1st Medical Battalion

1st Supply & Transp. Bn. | 121st Signal Battalion | 701st Maint. Battalion

1st Inf. Div. M.P. Company | 1st M.P. Company

Medals of America Press **13**

4th Infantry Division "Ivy" "Iron Horse"

Shoulder Sleeve Insignia

On a light khaki square, each side 2 inches *(5.08 cm)* in width overall and with one angle up, four green ivy leaves arranged per cross issuing from a small open circle *(one leaf in each angle of the square and the vertical and horizontal axis each $2\,^{11}/_{32}$ inches in length)* all within a $^{1}/_{8}$ inch light khaki border.

Symbolism

The four leaves allude to the numerical designation of the Division while the word "I-VY" as pronounced, suggests the characters used in the formation of the Roman numeral "IV." Ivy leaves are also symbolic of fidelity and tenacity. The shoulder sleeve insignia was originally approved for the 4th Division on 30 October 1918, without any background specified for the ivy leaf design. The design was embroidered on a square olive background *(color of the uniform)*. It was redesignated for the 4th Infantry Division effective 4 August 1943. On 2 July 1958, the design was changed to reflect the light khaki color background. The insignia was amended to add a symbolism on 1 April 1969.

Landed in RVN: 25 Sept. 1966
Left RVN: 7 Dec. 1970
Locale: Duc Pho, Pleiku, Kontum

Distinctive Unit Insignia

A gold color metal and enamel device, 1 inch in height overall consisting of an ivy leaf of green fimbriated gold above a scroll with the inscription "Steadfast and Loyal."

The ivy leaf is taken from the 4th Infantry Division shoulder sleeve insignia. The motto is associated with the Division.

Distinctive Unit Insignia

Fourth Infantry Division Assigned Infantry Battalions

| 1st, 2nd & 3rd Bn 8th Inf. Regt. | 1st, 2nd & 3rd Bn 12th Inf. Regt. | 1st Bn 14th Inf. Regt. | 2nd & 3rd Bn 22nd Inf. Regt. | 1st & 2nd Bn 35th Inf. Regt. |

Fourth Infantry Division Assigned Artillery Battalions

| 2nd Battalion 9th Fld. Arty Regt. | 5th Battalion 16th Fld. Arty Regt. | 6th Battalion 29th Fld. Arty Regt. | 4th Battalion 42nd Fld. Arty Regt. | 2nd Battalion 77th Fld. Arty Regt. |

★ Evolution of the 4th Infantry Division Patch

World War I Insignia	1920s	 1920s- 1938	 1938	 1958

1960	 Local made RVN	 1963	1970s	 Sub Units (LRRP)

4th Infantry Division Armor

 1st Bn, 34th Armor Regt.

 1st Bn, 69th Armor Regt.

 1st Sqn, 10th Cav Regt.

4th Infantry Division Support

 4th Engr. Bn.

 704th Maint. Battalion

 4th Medical Battalion

⭐ 1st Brigade, 5th Infantry Division "Red Diamond"

Landed in RVN: 25 July 1968
Left RVN: 27 Aug. 1971
Locale: Quang Tri

Shoulder Sleeve Insignia

A red diamond *(a rhombus)* with vertical axis 2 $\frac{1}{2}$ inches *(6.35 cm)* and horizontal axis 1 $\frac{1}{2}$ inches *(3.81 cm)*.

Symbolism

The insignia was adopted by the Division upon its arrival in France. The color red was selected as a compliment to the then Commanding General whose branch of the service was the Artillery. The *"ace of diamonds"* was selected from the trade name *"Diamond dye - it never runs."* The red diamond represents a well-known problem in bridge building, it is made up of two adjacent isosceles triangles which made for the greatest strength. The Division's nickname is *"Red Diamond."*

Distinctive Unit Insignia

It is reported that the Division was latterly known among the Germans opposed to it as the *"Red Tigers"* and the *"Red Devils."*

The shoulder sleeve insignia was originally approved for 5th Division on 20 October 1918. It was amended on 11 October 1922, to correct the wording of the description. On 25 May 1943, the insignia was redesignated for the 5th Infantry Division and amended to include the symbolism of the design.

Distinctive Unit Insignia

A silver color metal and enamel insignia 1 $\frac{1}{8}$ inches *(2.86 cm)* in height consisting of a red diamond shaped spearhead pointed upwards and bisecting a blue wave, encircling the base of the spearhead a silver scroll inscribed with the words "WE WILL" in black.

Symbolism

The design symbolizes the piercing of the German Army's Meuse River defenses by the men of the 5th Division in World War I, an achievement which caused the organization to be known as the Meuse Division and gave them their Red Diamond emblem. The operation was described by General Pershing as "one of the most brilliant military feats in the history of the American Army in France."

 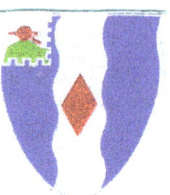  

| 1st Bn | 1st Bn | 1st Bn | 5th Bn. |
| 11th Inf. Regt. | 61th Inf. Regt. | 77th Armor Regt.. | 4th Fld. Arty Regt. |

⭐ 3rd Brigade, 9TH Infantry Division "Go Devils"

Separated from 9th Div. in RVN: 26 July 1969
Left RVN: 11 Oct. 1970
Locale: Tan An

The 3rd Brigade was separated from the 9th Infantry Division in July 1969 and assigned to the 25th division becoming the only remaining Brigade of the 9th infantry division in Vietnam.

Unauthorized

9th Infantry Division "Old Reliables"

Shoulder Sleeve Insignia

An olive drab disc 2 $^5/_8$ inches in diameter overall charged with a double quatrefoil horizontally divided into two equal halves red uppermost and blue, with a white center.

Symbolism

The double quatrefoil, which is a heraldic mark of cadency for the ninth son, has been made red and blue, the designating colors of an Infantry Division headquarters flag; the white center is in the color of the numerals for divisional flags.

Distinctive Unit Insignia

Background

The shoulder sleeve insignia was originally approved for the 9th Division on 18 November 1925. It was redesignated for the 9th Infantry Division effective 1 August 1942. The insignia was amended to revise the dimensions of the design to provide for an over edge stitching on 27 February 1970.

Landed in RVN: 16 Dec.1966
Left RVN: 27 Aug 1969
Locale: Dong Tam, Tan An

Distinctive Unit Insignia

A metal and enamel insignia 1 $^1/_8$ inches in height consisting of a golden disc charged with a blue fleur-de-lis and radiating nine gold rays, all but the one at top center contained by a red crescent. The high points of the 9th Division's World War II history are represented in the following manner: The red crescent is for the Tunisian campaign; the nine rays of the sun denote the unit's numerical designation, and likewise refer to the campaign in Sicily; the gold disc in center is for Central Europe and the fleur-de-lis thereon represents service in Northern France. The distinctive unit insignia was approved on 2 February 1966.

9th Infantry Division Assigned Infantry and Artillery Battalions

PRO PATRIA

6th Bn
31st Inf. Regt.

2nd, 3rd & 4th Bn
39th Inf. Regt.

2nd, 3rd & 4th
Bn 47th Inf. Regt.

TO THE UTMOST EXTENT OF OUR POWER

2nd, 3rd & 5th Bn
60th Inf. Regt.

2nd Battalion
4th Fld. Arty. Regt.

ON TIME

1th Battalion
11th Fld. Arty.Regt.

WE SUPPORT

3rd Battalion
34th Fld. Arty. Regt.

PERFORMANCE ABOVE ALL

1st Battalion, 84th
Fld. Arty. Regt.

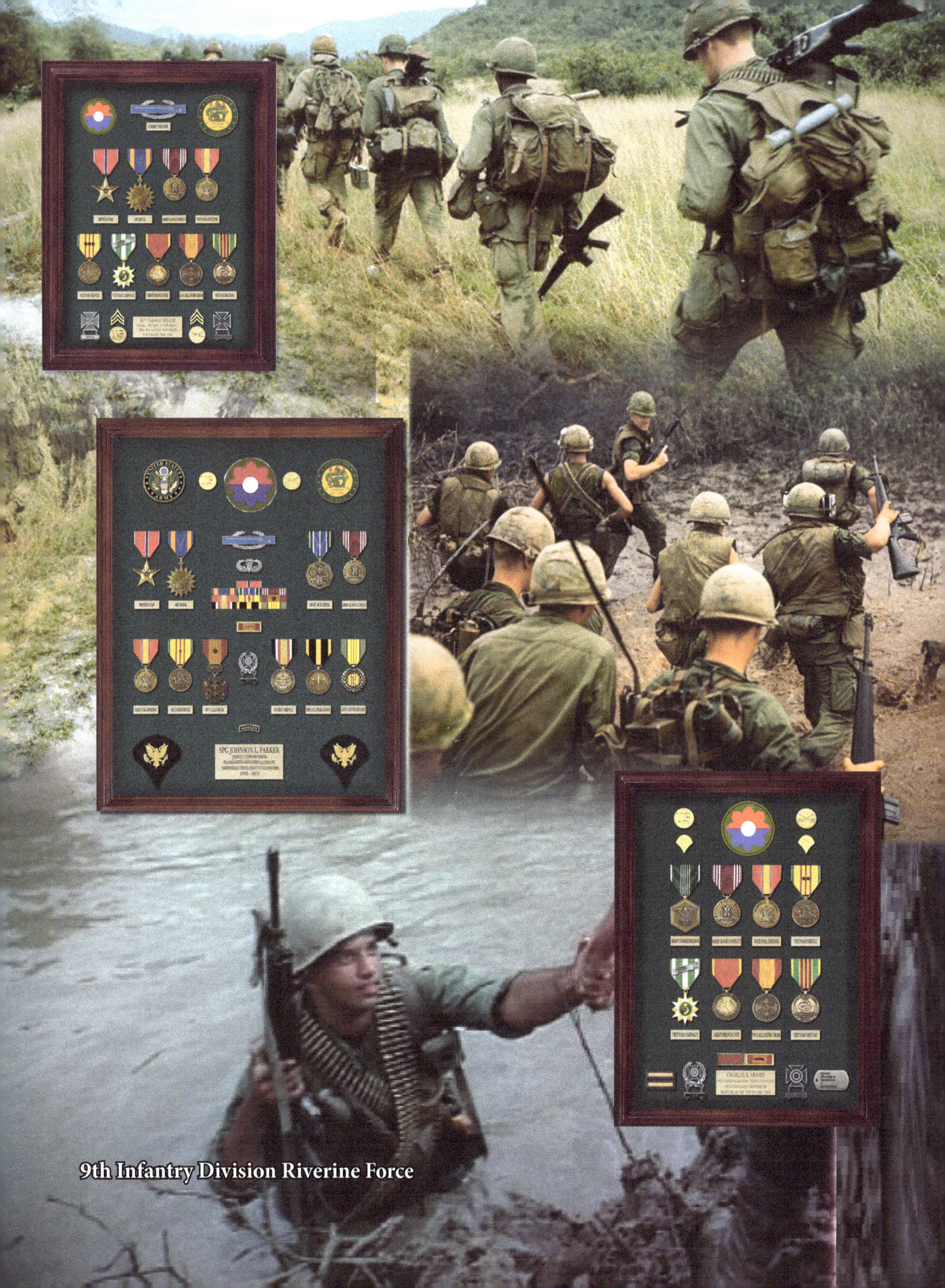
SPC JOHNSON L. PARKER
9th Infantry Division Riverine Force

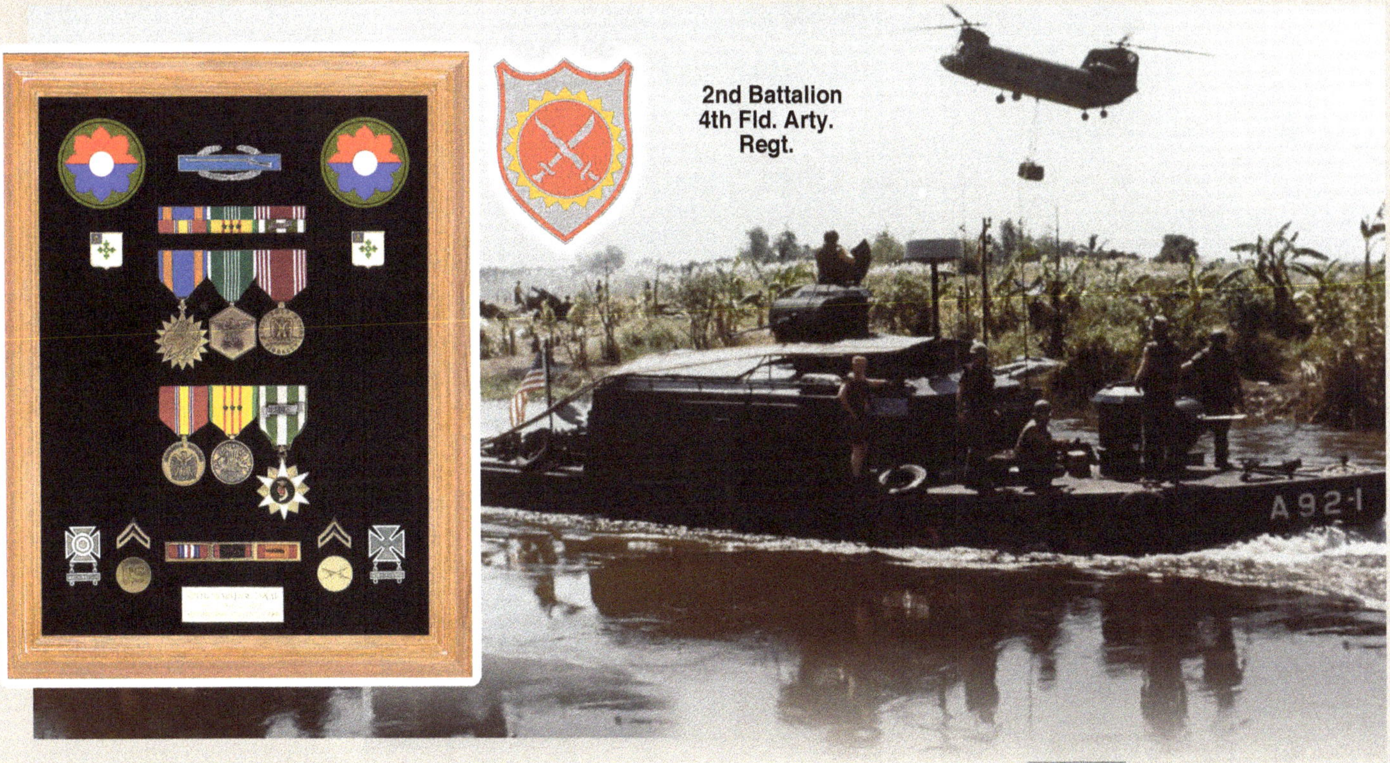
A92-1

2nd Battalion
4th Fld. Arty.
Regt.

3rd & 4th
Bn 47th Inf. Regt.

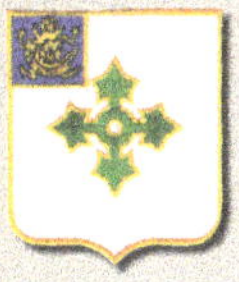

9th Infantry Division Riverine Force

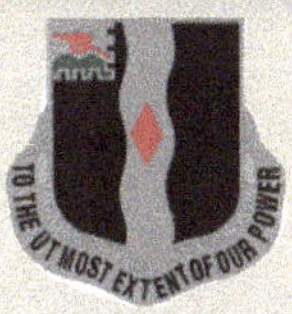
TO THE UTMOST EXTENT OF OUR POWER

3rd Bn
60th Inf. Regt.

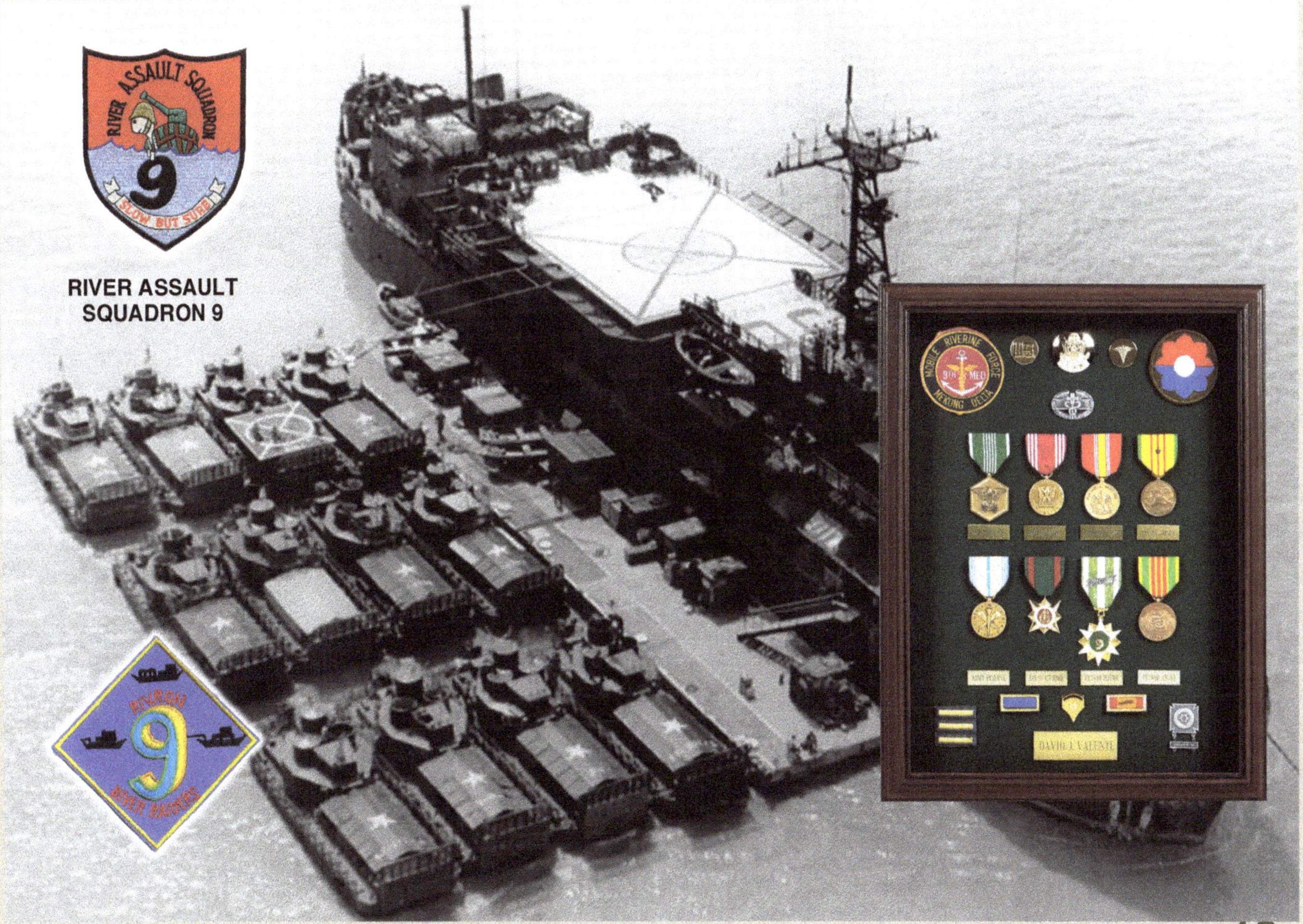
RIVER ASSAULT SQUADRON
9
SLOW BUT SURE

RIVER ASSAULT
SQUADRON 9

23rd Infantry Division "Americal"

Shoulder Sleeve Insignia

On a blue Norman shield 2 $^{5}/_{8}$ inches *(6.67 cm)* in height and 2 $^{1}/_{8}$ inches *(5.40 cm)* in width, four white stars of varying sizes all slightly tipped to the dexter, arranged to represent the Southern Cross.

Symbolism

The four white stars on the blue field are symbolic of the Southern Cross under which the organization has served.

The shoulder sleeve insignia was originally approved for the Americal Division on 20 December 1943. It was redesignated for the 23rd Infantry Division on 4 November 1954.

AMERICAL
Distinctive Unit Insignia

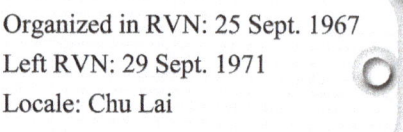

Distinctive Unit Insignia

A gold color metal and enamel device 1 $^{3}/_{8}$ inches *(3.49 cm)* in height overall consisting of a blue saltire with each arm charged at its terminus with a white five-pointed star, the vertical axis of each star diagonally from upper left to lower right, in front of a horizontal gold anchor, crown to left and gold cable passing through the anchor ring and behind the saltire arms, and a vertical stylized red arrowhead between and touching the two upper arms of the saltire and surmounting a gold sun with gold rays extending above the saltire, overall a gold unsheathed sword, point to top and within the confines of the arrowhead, the ends of the guard between and conjoined with the inner edges of the two lower arms of the saltire and the pommel resting on a continuation of the gold anchor cable, the areas to each side of the blade where it extends below the saltire and the hilt above the anchor cable all in red, all other areas between the anchor, anchor cable and arrowhead and the saltire of gold stippled, all above a gold motto scroll, the ends terminating at the lower arms of the saltire, bearing the inscription

Organized in RVN: 25 Sept. 1967
Left RVN: 29 Sept. 1971
Locale: Chu Lai

"AMERICAL" in blue letters, the area between the scroll and anchor cable of gold stippled.

Symbolism

The saltire *(or cross of St. Andrew)* alludes to New Caledonia in the Southwest Pacific where the Division was created and first activated 27 May 1942, and with its blue color *(for Infantry)* and four white stars forms a "Southern Cross" and refers to the Division's shoulder sleeve insignia *(approved 20 December 1943)* and the area in which the Division initially served. The four stars (the brightest in the Southern Cross constellation) also allude to the four campaigns *(Guadalcanal, Northern Solomons, Leyte and Southern Philippines)* of World War II in which the Division participated. The anchor refers to the Presidential Unit Citation *(Navy)* awarded the Division for Guadalcanal and the red arrowhead and Philippine sun for the assault landing, Southern Philippines, and the award of the Philippine Presidential Unit Citation *(17 October 1944 to 4 July 1945)*. The unsheathed sword with point to top refers to Vietnam where the Division was recently activated. In view of the Division's origin and outstanding service in World War II and inasmuch as it was one of the few U.S. Army Divisions to bear a name instead of a number, the Division's former name "Americal" has been taken as a motto, the association with that name being both inspirational and of historical military significance.

11th Inf. Brigade

196th Inf. Brigade

198th Inf Brigade

★ 25th Infantry Division "Tropic Lightning"

Shoulder Sleeve Insignia

On a red taro leaf, 2 7/8 inches *(7.30 cm)* in height, and 2 inches *(5.08 cm)* in width at the widest point, with stem up, surrounded by a 1/8 inch *(.32 cm)* yellow border, a yellow lightning flash per pale 1 13/16 inches *(4.60 cm)* in height.

Landed in RVN: 28 Mar. 1966
Left RVN: 8 Dec. 1970
Locale: Pleiku, Tay Ninh, Saigon

Symbolism

The taro leaf is indicative of the descent of the 25th Division from the Hawaiian Division, while the lightning flash is representative of the manner in which the Division performs its allotted assignments.

The shoulder sleeve insignia was authorized on 25 September 1944.

Distinctive Unit Insignia

Distinctive Unit Insignia

Centered on a black volcano emitting a gold cloud a vertical lightning flash divided red above and gold below all enclosed by a pair of green palm branches with stems crossed in base and leaves terminating at either side of the cloud above.

The lightning flash, adopted from the shoulder sleeve insignia of the 25th Infantry Division and the enclosing palm branches allude to the Division nickname *"Tropic Lightning"*. The erupting volcano is an allusion to the State of Hawaii. The distinctive insignia was approved on 21 April 1965. It was amended on 18 May 1972, to correct the nickname of the 25th Infantry Division in the symbolism.

| 1st Bn. 5th Inf. Regt. | 4th Bn. 9th Inf. Regt. | 2nd Bn. 12th Inf. Regt. | 2nd Bn. 14th Inf. Regt. | 3rd Bn. 22nd Inf. Regt. |

| 4th Bn. 23rd Inf. Regt. | 2nd Bn., 27th Inf. Regt. | 1st & 2nd Bn. 35th Inf. Regt. | 2nd Bn., 34th Armor Regt. | 1st Bn., 69th Armor Regt. |

| 1nd Battalion 8th Fld. Arty. Regt. | 2nd Battalion 9th Fld. Arty. Regt. | 1th Battalion 11th Fld. Arty. Regt. | 3rd Battalion 13th Fld. Arty. Regt. | 2nd Battalion 77th Fld. Arty. Regt. |

82nd Airborne Division "All American"

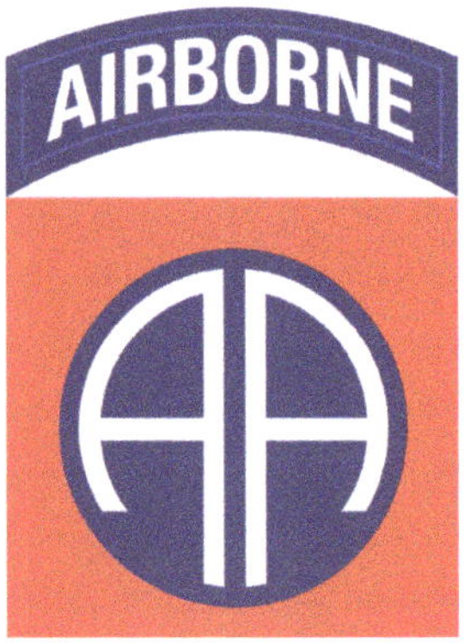
AIRBORNE

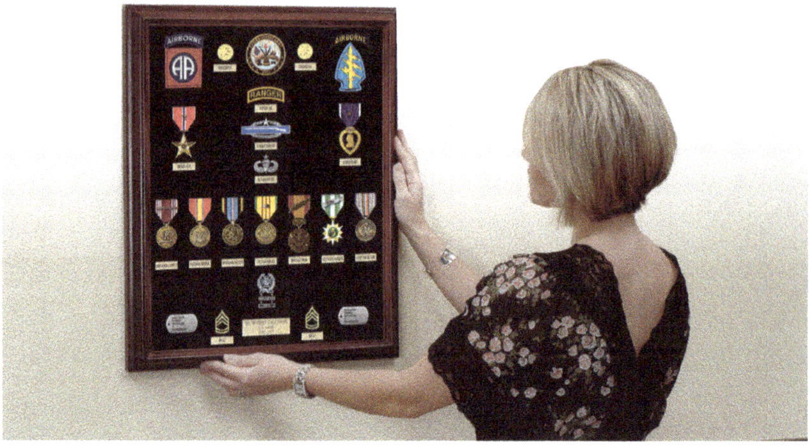

Shoulder Sleeve Insignia

Upon a red square 2 $^{3}/_{8}$ inches *(6.03 cm)* on a side a blue disc 1 $^{3}/_{4}$ inches *(4.45 cm)* in diameter with the letters AA in white. The inner elements of the two A's vertical lines and the outer elements arcs of a circle 1 $^{3}/_{8}$ inches *(3.49 cm)* in diameter, elements of the letters $^{1}/_{8}$ inch *(.32 cm)* in width. Attached immediately above the square is a blue tab with the word "AIRBORNE" in white.

Symbolism

The double "A" refers to the nickname "All American Division" adopted by the organization in France during World War I.

The shoulder sleeve insignia was approved for the 82nd Division by the Adjutant General, American Expeditionary Forces on 21 October 1918 and was confirmed by The Adjutant General on 8 July 1922. The insignia was redesignated for the 82nd Airborne Division and an "AIRBORNE" tab authorized on 31 August 1942. on 1 March 1949.

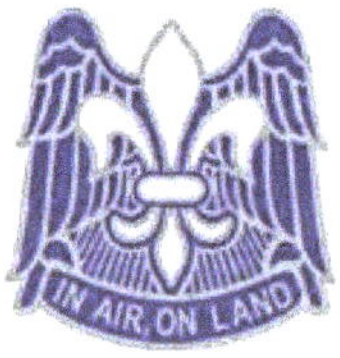
IN AIR, ON LAND

Landed in RVN: 18 Feb.1968
Left RVN: 11 Dec.1969
Locale: Hue, Phu Bai, Phu Loi, Saigon

Distinctive Unit Insignia

A silver color metal and enamel device 1 $^{1}/_{8}$ inches *(2.86 cm)* in height overall consisting of pair of blue stylized wings, tips down surmounted by a white fleur-de-lis supported by a blue scroll inscribed, *"IN AIR, ON LAND"* in silver color metal letters.

The fleur-de-lis is representative of the battle honors earned in France during World War I. The wings are symbolic of the Division's mission. The motto is expressive of the personnel of the organization either on land or in the air.

The distinctive unit insignia was approved on 23 October 1942. It was redesignated for the Command and Control Battalion, 82nd Airborne Division on 21 April 1958. It was redesignated for the non-color bearing units of the 82nd Airborne Division on 6 June 1966. The insignia was cancelled and a distinctive unit insignia of the same design as the shoulder sleeve was authorized on 31 July 1990. The original insignia was reinstated on 21 May 1998.

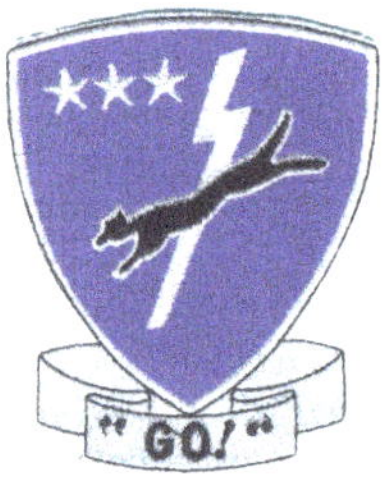
"GO!"

505th Abn. Inf. Regt.

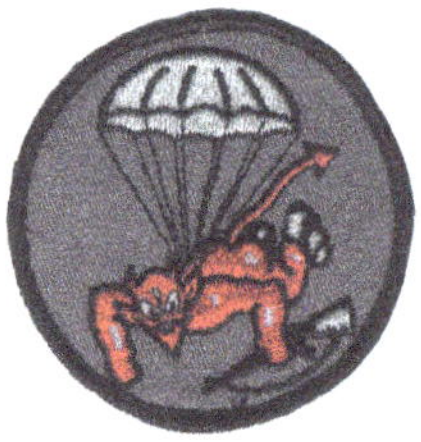

508th Abn. Inf. Regt.

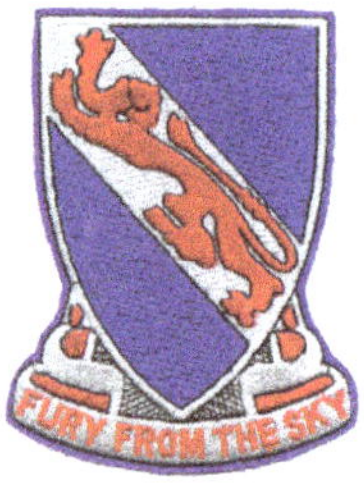
FURY FROM THE SKY

508th Abn. Inf. Regt.

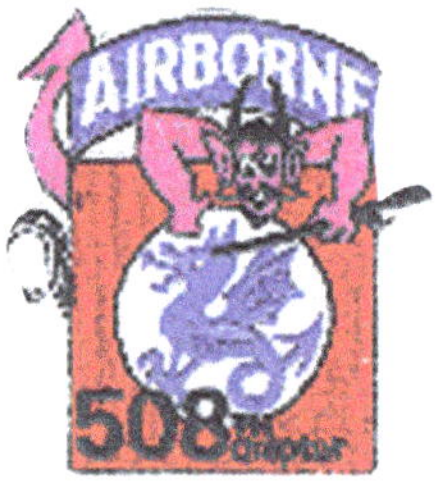
AIRBORNE
508

508th Abn. Inf. Regt.

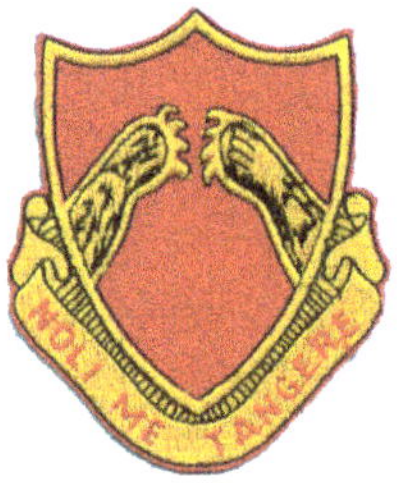
NOLI ME TANGERE

321st Abn Field. Arty. Bn.

101st Airborne Division "Screaming Eagles"

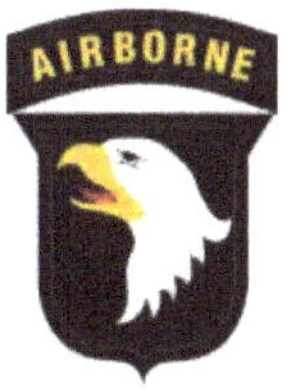
AIRBORNE

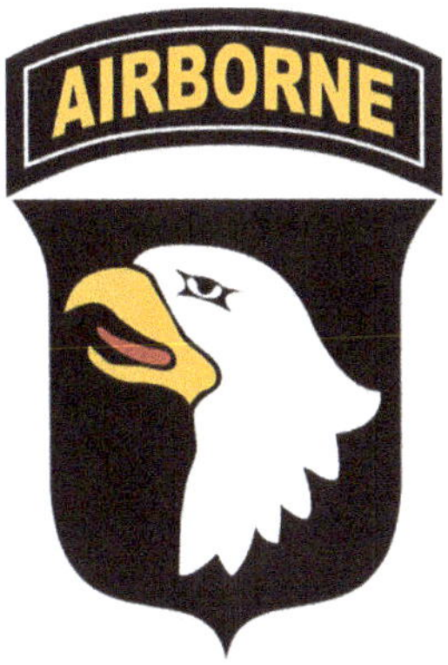
AIRBORNE

Shoulder Sleeve Insignia

On a shield $2\,^{1}/_{2}$ inches *(6.35 cm)* in height overall, Sable the head of a bald eagle Proper. Attached above the insignia is a Black tab inscribed *"AIRBORNE"* in Yellow.

Symbolism

The design is based on one of the Civil War traditions of the State of Wisconsin, this State being the territory of the original 101st Division. The eagle alludes to *"Old Abe,"* the famous war eagle carried into combat during the Civil War by the 8th Wisconsin Infantry Regiment.

The shoulder sleeve insignia was originally approved for the 101st Division on 23 May 1923. It was redesignated for the 101st Airborne Division on 28 August 1942. It was redesignated for the 101st Air Cavalry Division on 5 August 1968. The insignia was redesignated for the 101st Airborne Division *(Airmobile)* on 10 September 1968. It was amended to update the description and correct the symbolism on 8 February 2006. *(TIOH Drawing Number A-1-148).*

Distinctive Unit Insignia

On and over a medium blue disc, a black demi-eagle with white head, wing details, eye and beak gold, in downward flight issuing from a white cloud in sinister base, all above a gold scroll bearing the motto *"RENDEZVOUS WITH DESTINY"* in black letters.

Landed in RVN: 19 Nov. 1967
Left RVN:10 Mar. 1972
Locale: Phan Rang, Quang Tri, Thua Thien

Symbolism

The design was suggested by the Division's authorized shoulder sleeve insignia. The black eagle alluding to *"Old Abe,"* an actual eagle carried into combat during the Civil War by one of the regiments from the State of Wisconsin, the territory of the original 101st Division. The eagle issuing in downward flight from the cloud refers to the airborne classification of the Division. The motto, *"Rendezvous With Destiny"* has been the motto of the Division since its founding.

Background

The distinctive unit insignia was originally approved for the Command and Control Battalion, 101st Airborne Division on 21 April 1958. It was redesignated for the non-color bearing units of the 101st Airborne Division on 24 July 1968. It was redesignated for the 101st Air Cavalry Division on 5 August 1968. The insignia was redesignated for the non-color bearing units of the 101st Airborne Division *(Airmobile)* and amended to include a symbolism on 10 September 1968. It was amended to correct the symbolism on 8 February 2006.

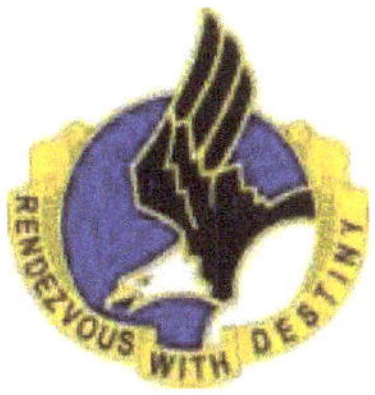
RENDEZVOUS WITH DESTINY

Distinctive Unit Insignia

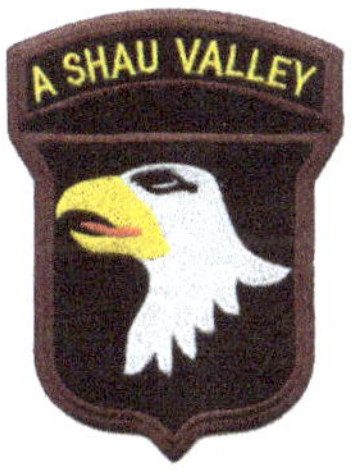
A SHAU VALLEY

101st Abn Div. A Shau Valley

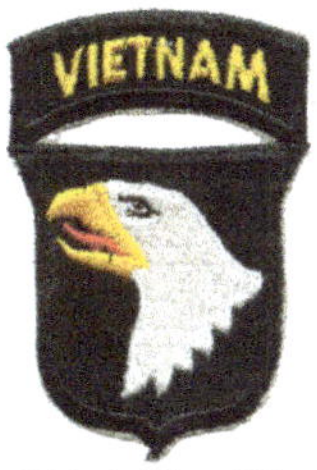
VIETNAM

101st Abn Div. Vietnam

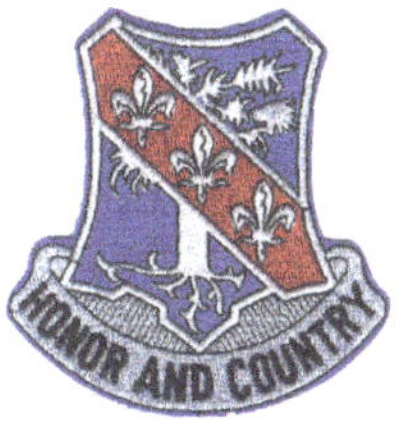
HONOR AND COUNTRY

327th Abn. Inf. Regt.

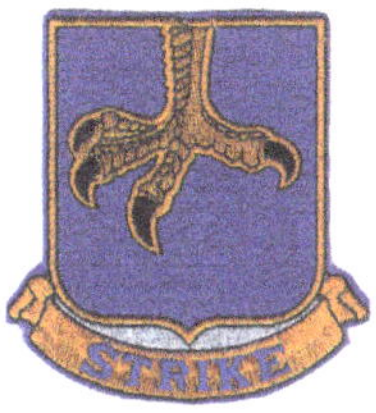
STRIKE

502nd Abn. Inf. Regt.

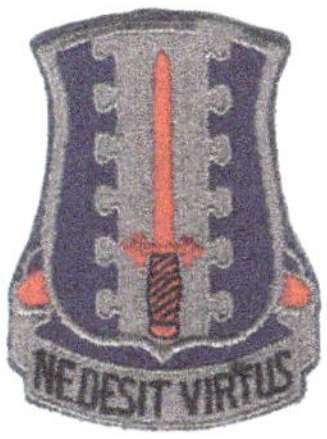
NE DESIT VIRTUS

187th Abn. Inf. Regt.

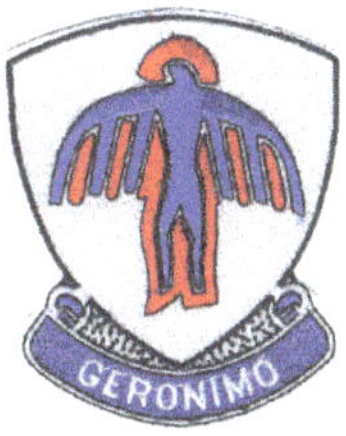
GERONIMO

501st Abn. Inf. Regt.

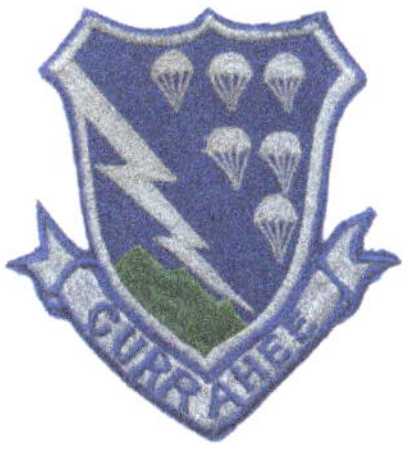
CURRAHEE

506th Abn. Inf. Regt.

11th Armored Cavalry Regiment "The Blackhorse Regiment"

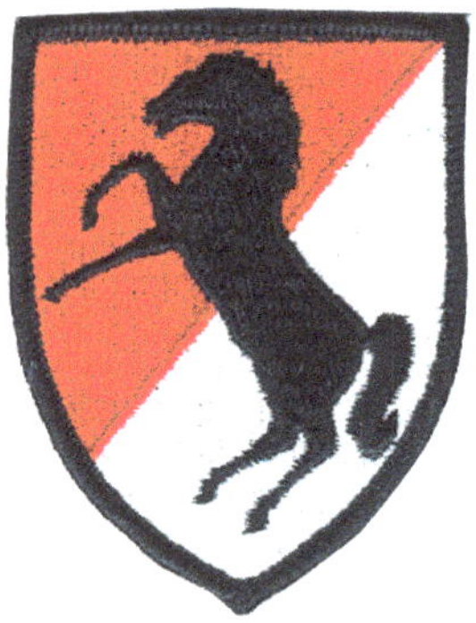

Landed in RVN: 8 Sept. 1966
Left RVN: 9 March 1971
Locale: Tay Ninh

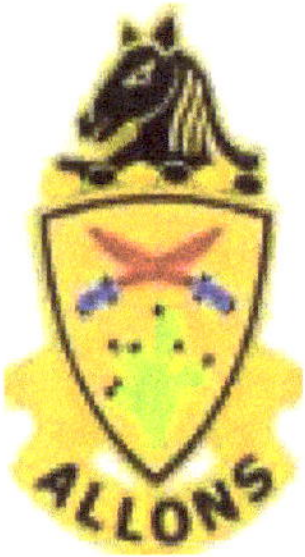
ALLONS

Distinctive Unit Insignia

Shoulder Sleeve Insignia

On a shield $2\frac{3}{4}$ inches in width overall divided diagonally from upper right to lower left, the upper portion red and the lower portion white, a rearing black horse facing to the left all within a $\frac{1}{8}$ inch black border.

Symbolism

The colors red and white are the traditional Cavalry colors and the rearing black horse alludes to the "Black Horse" nickname of the 11th Armored Cavalry. This insignia was approved on 1 May 1967.

Distinctive Unit Insignia

A gold color metal and enamel device $1\frac{1}{4}$ inches in height overall blazoned as follows: within a shield two bolos crosswise with blue hilts with a cactus below. A black horse's head is on the crest of the shield. Attached below and to the sides of the device a Gold scroll inscribed *"ALLONS"* in Black letters.

Symbolism

The regiment was organized in 1901 and saw service in the Philippines. This is indicated by the crossed bolos with red blades and blue hilts. The regiment rendered very good service on the Mexican Border in 1916 and this is indicated by the cactus. The regimental colors black and yellow are shown by the shield and the black border within the edge and by the color of the crest which shows against the yellow regimental flag. The motto translates to *"Come."*

This insignia was originally approved for the 11th Cavalry Regiment on 6 January 1925. It was redesignated for the 11th Armored Cavalry Regiment on 26 November 1951.

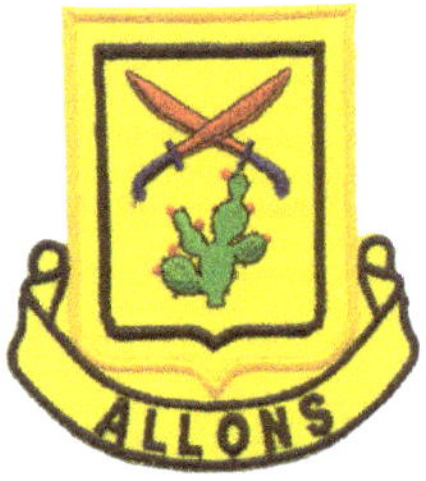
ALLONS

11th A.C.R.

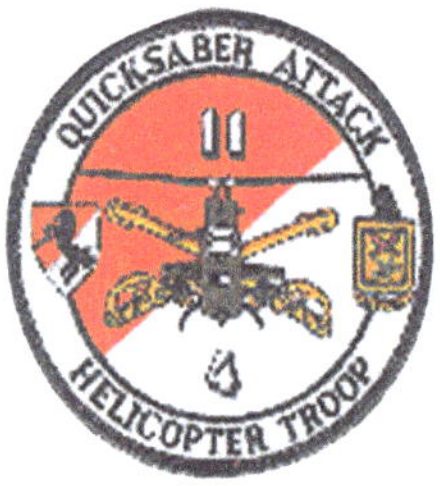
QUICKSABER ATTACK
11
HELICOPTER TROOP

11th A.C.R. 4th Bn.

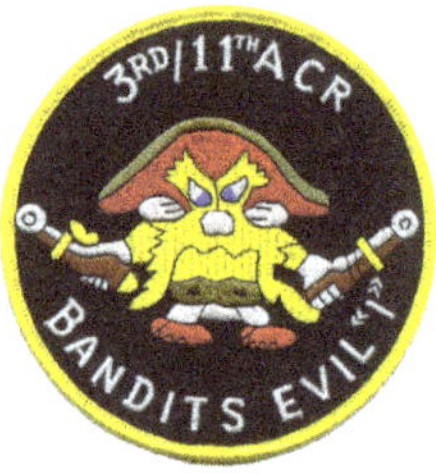
3RD/11TH ACR
BANDITS EVIL "I"

11th A.C.R.

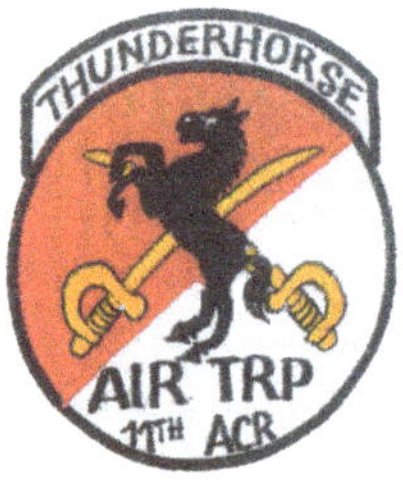
THUNDERHORSE
AIR TRP
11TH ACR

11th A.C.R. Air Troop

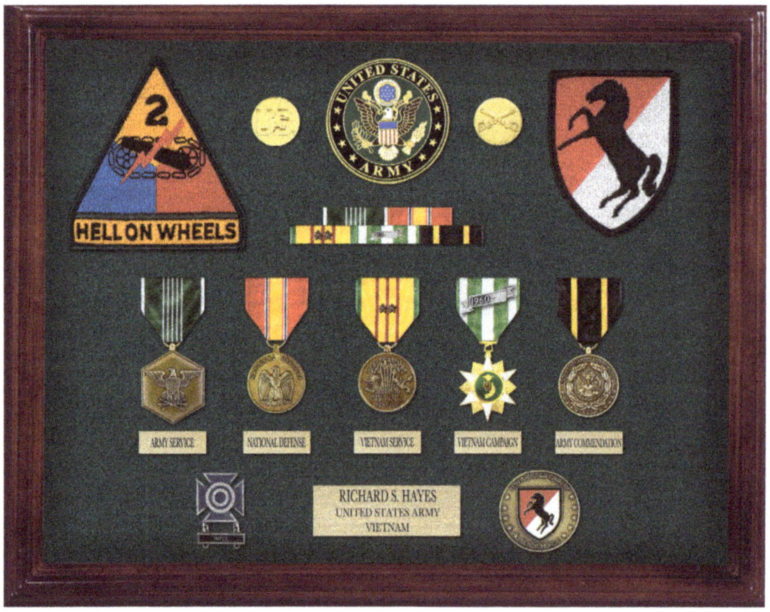
HELL ON WHEELS
UNITED STATES ARMY
ARMY SERVICE
NATIONAL DEFENSE
VIETNAM SERVICE
VIETNAM CAMPAIGN
ARMY COMMENDATION
RICHARD S. HAYES
UNITED STATES ARMY
VIETNAM

11th Infantry Brigade "Brave Rifles"

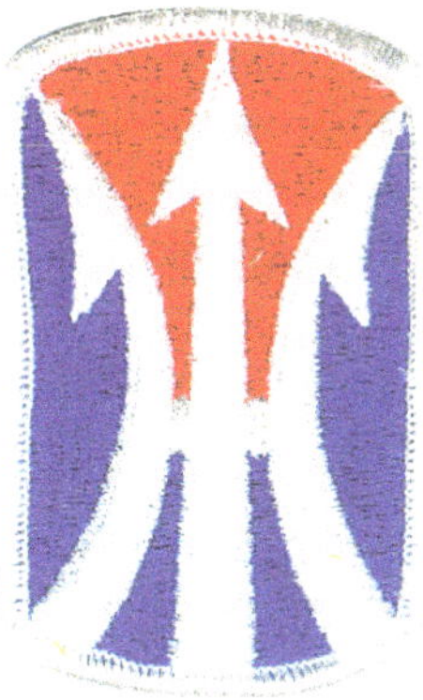

Shoulder Sleeve Insignia

On a shield, oblong in shape and arched at both ends, 3 inches in height and 2 inches in width overall, within a $^1/_8$ inch white border, a vertical white arrow between 2 inwardly curved white arrows. The upper area between the curved arrows is red and the balance is blue.

The sweeping prongs simulate the elements of the unit in attack and in resembling a trident also allude to amphibious assault. The shoulder sleeve insignia was approved on 28 July 1966.

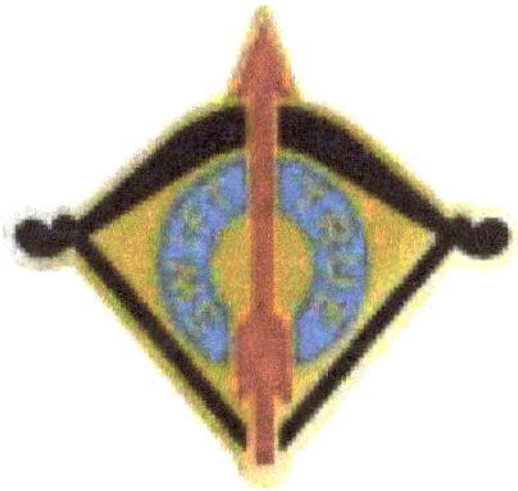

Distinctive Unit Insignia

Distinctive Unit Insignia

A metal and enamel device 1 $^1/_8$ inches in height *(arrow wise)* and 1 $^1/_4$ inches in width (bow wise) consisting of a gold colored metal base with a black bow, bent and stringed black and a red arrow, barbed and feathered red, nocked and drawn up to the point, the shaft passing over a light blue annulet bearing on the dexter portion the word *"SWIFT"* and on the sinister portion the word *"TRUE"* reading from left to right, all in gold color letters.

Landed in RVN: 19 Dec. 1967
Left RVN: 13 Nov. 1971
Locale: Duc Pho, The Loi

The bow with arrow refers to the mobility and striking power of the organization, further emphasized by the words *"SWIFT"* and *"TRUE."* The bow and arrow also allude to the silence and stealth of movement and surprise attack, the arrow, straight and true, implying constant advance and the overcoming of all obstacles. The red arrow, the Indian symbol of war, is also emblematic of fire power. The annulet symbolizes fidelity and tenacity of purpose. The color black signifies wisdom and prudence, the red, courage; the blue *(light blue for Infantry),* loyalty and faith; and the gold; inspiration, zeal and achievement. The distinctive unit insignia was approved on 27 July 1966.

For its service in Vietnam, the entire 11th was awarded the Republic of Vietnam Cross of Gallantry with Palm for 1969 and 1970, while the HHC received the award for 1968–1969 and 1971.

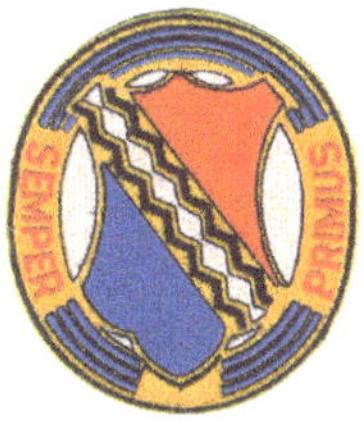
SEMPER
PRIMUS

1st Inf. Regt.

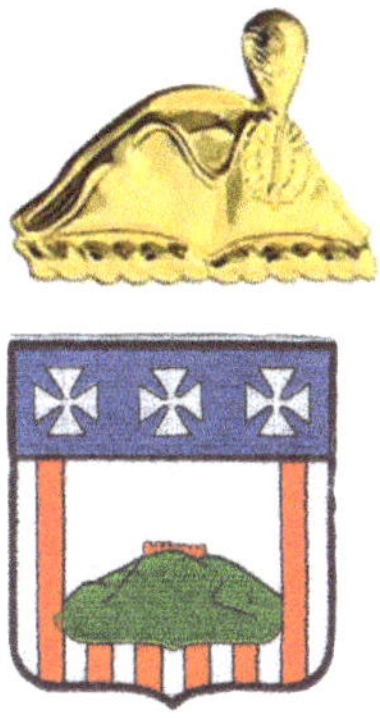

3rd Inf. Regt.

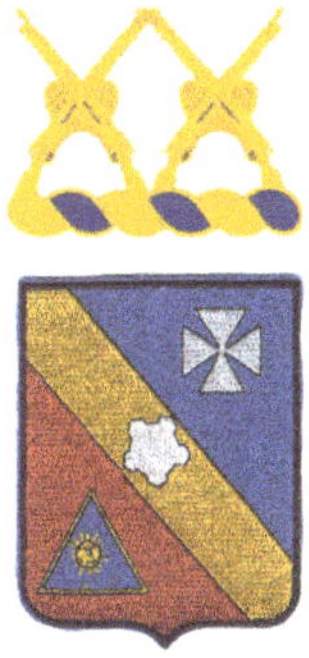

20th Inf. Regt.

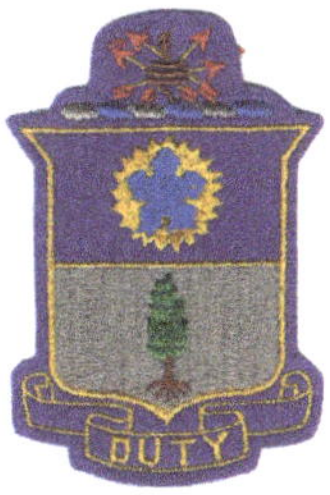
DUTY

21st Inf. Regt.

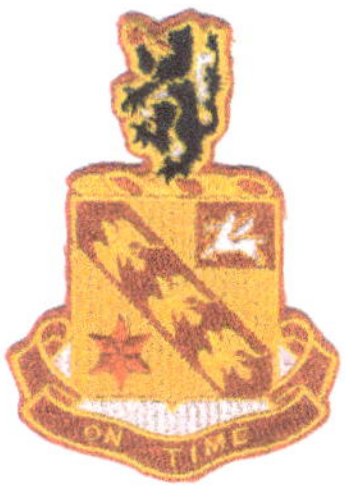
ON TIME

11th Fld. Arty. Bn.

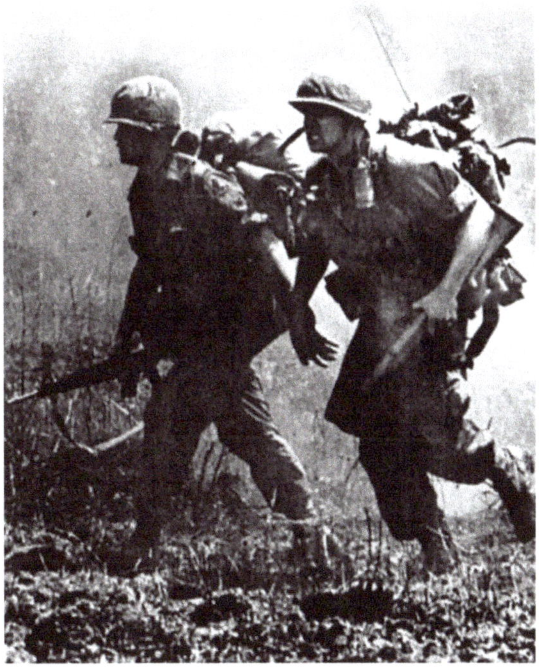

173d Airborne Brigade "Sky Soldiers"

Distinctive Unit Insignia

Landed in RVN: 7 May 1965
Left RVN: 25 Aug. 1971
Locale: Bien Hoa, An Khe, Tuy Hoa, Bong Son

Shoulder Sleeve Insignia

On a blue silhouetted right cylinder 3 inches (7.62 cm) in height and 2 inches (5.08 cm) in width overall within a $1/8$ inch (.32 cm) white border a vertical white wing in flight, the ulna (lower end) extended and hooked around a red bayonet. Attached above the insignia is a blue tab inscribed "AIRBORNE" in white.

The bayonet is used to refer to the brigade being borne by the wing which alludes to the brigade's airborne status. Red, white and blue are the national colors.

The shoulder sleeve insignia was originally approved on 13 May 1963. It was amended to correct the dimensions on 29 July 1963. The insignia was amended to include the tab and update the description on 26 April 2000. It was redesignated for the 173d Airborne Brigade Combat Team on 11 October 2006.

Distinctive Unit Insignia

A silver color metal and enamel device $1\ 1/4$ inches (3.18 cm) in height overall consisting of a semi-circle divided into three sections each with a concave base. The outer two sections are silver and the center section is red. A vertical unsheathed silver sword points to the base with the hilt resting on the red section of the semi-circle lower edge of the guard coinciding with the concave base and the ends conjoined with the silver sections the blade between two lightning flashes converging toward the point of the blade. The flashes are parallel and enclose two narrow inclined silver lines starting at the diameter of the semi-circle and meeting beneath the point of the sword. The area enclosed in blue above a stylized motto scroll, the ends simulating wings and terminating at the base of the semi-circle, bearing the inscription "SKY SOLDIERS" in blue letters.

The simulated parachute and stylized wings refer to the airborne mission of the Brigade. The unsheathed sword, point to base (implying from sky to ground) and the hilt against the red section of the parachute canopy, alludes to the combat assault jump made by the Brigade in February 1967, the first such jump made by any unit in Vietnam indicated by the "V" formed by the two lightning flashes on the V-shaped silver edged blue area. The single sword also alludes to other Brigade "firsts" such as first American ground unit in Vietnam, first in War Zones C and D and first in the Iron Triangle. The lightning flashes are also symbolic of the Brigade's striking power and surprise and rapidity of movement. The numerical designation of the Brigade can be readily simulated by various combinations of the design elements, i.e., the sword indicating one (1), the sum of the wings, the two lightning flashes and the three sections of the parachute canopy being Seven (7) and the latter by itself also being used for three (3). The distinctive unit insignia was originally approved for the 173rd Airborne Brigade on 10 August 1967. The insignia was redesignated for the 173rd Airborne Brigade Combat Team with the description updated on 11 October 2006.

503rd Abn. Inf. Regt.

503rd Abn. Inf. Regt.

319th Abn. Field. Arty. Bn.

17th Cavalry Regiment

173rd ABN.BDE. L.R.R.P.

Shoulder Sleeve Insignia and Crest of the U.S. Army Vietnam

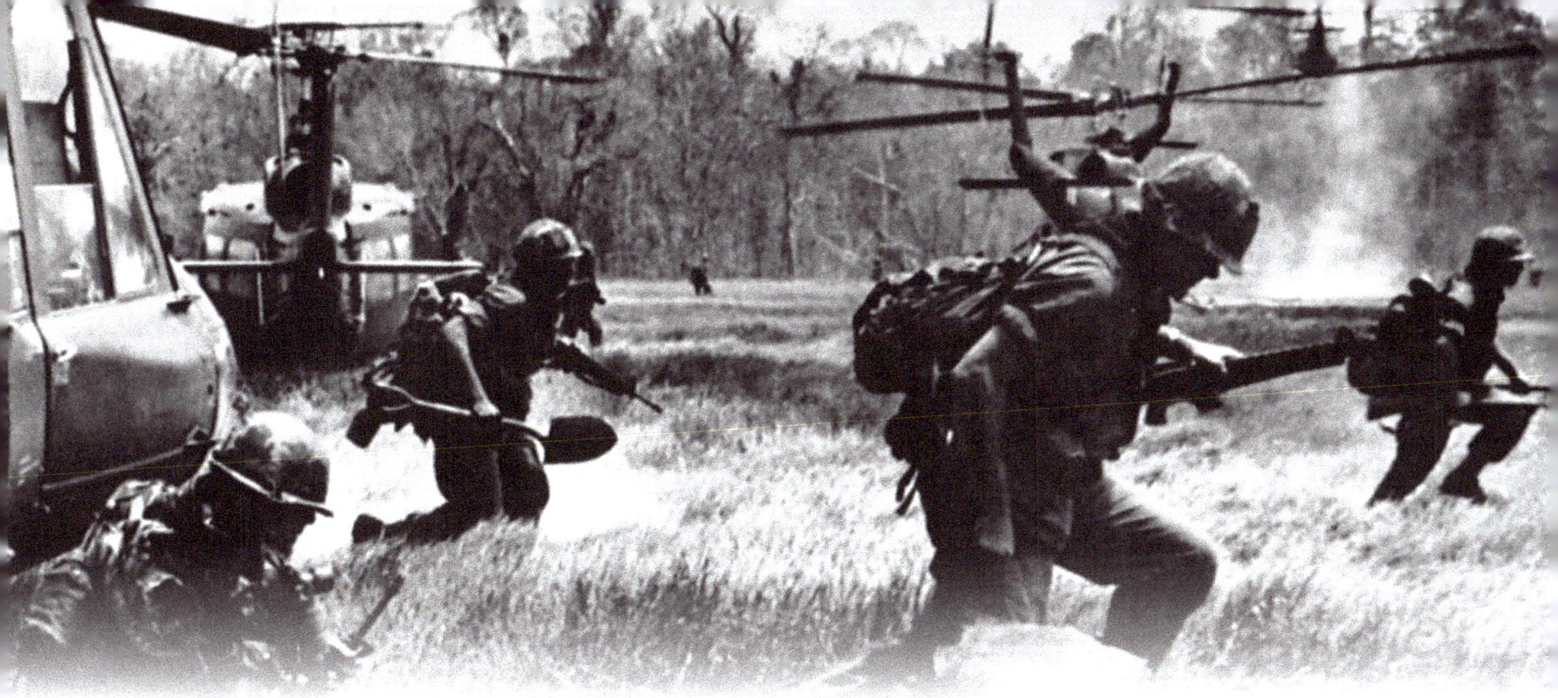

196th Infantry Brigade "Chargers"

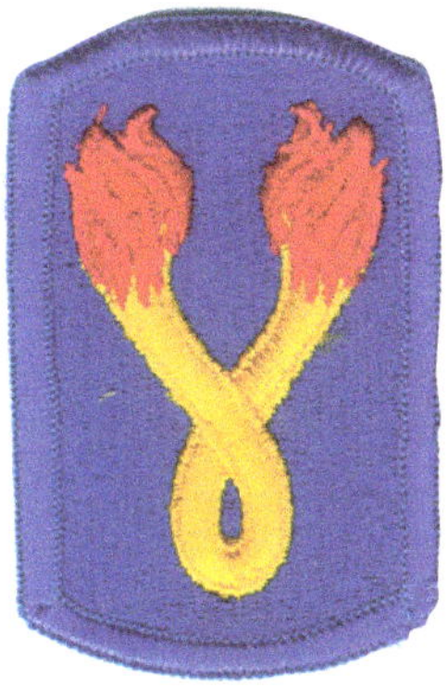

Shoulder Sleeve Insignia

On an oblong blue shield at both ends, 3 inches (7.62 cm) in height and 2 inches (5.08 cm) in width overall a yellow double headed match crossed and looped at the bottom and enflamed at both ends.

The color blue is used to denote Infantry. The yellow and red allude to the Cavalry and the Artillery. The double headed match, used during the days of the matchlock musket, was lighted at both ends to insure readiness.

The shoulder sleeve insignia was approved on 29 October 1965.

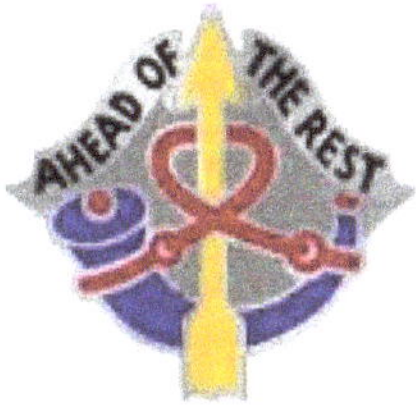
AHEAD OF THE REST
Distinctive Unit Insignia

Distinctive Unit Insignia

A silver color metal and enamel device $1\ ^1/_8$ inches (2.86 cm) in width overall consisting of a blue powder horn with a red string looped about a yellow vertical arrow, the arrowhead on the center fold of a silver scroll arched from the ends of the powder horn simulating a bow, between the motto "AHEAD OF THE REST" in black.

The powder horn, an American symbol for readiness of a rifleman, is used to denote the organization's preparedness. The arrow and the bow-like scroll refer to the bow and arrow on the seal of the state of Massachusetts alluding to the home area of the Brigade. The colors are for the three basic combat arms of an AIRSTRIKE Brigade: Blue, Infantry; red, Artillery; yellow, Armor.

The distinctive unit insignia was approved on 1 March 1966.

Landed in RVN: 26 Aug. 1966
Left RVN: 29 June 1972
Locale: Tay Ninh, Chu Lai, Kam Ky, Phong Dien, Hoi An, Da Nang

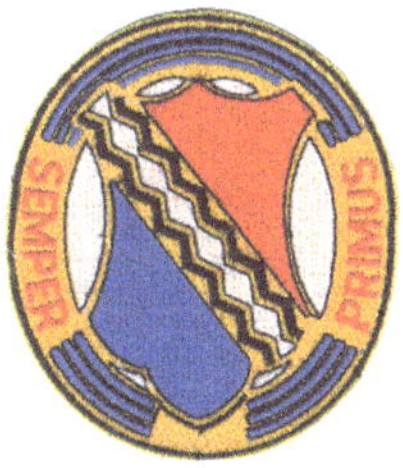
SEMPER PRIMUS
1st Inf. Regt.

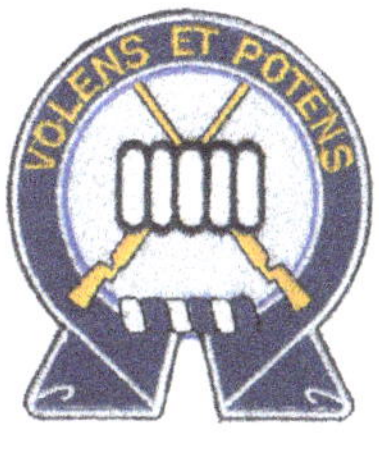
VOLENS ET POTENS
7th Inf. Regt.

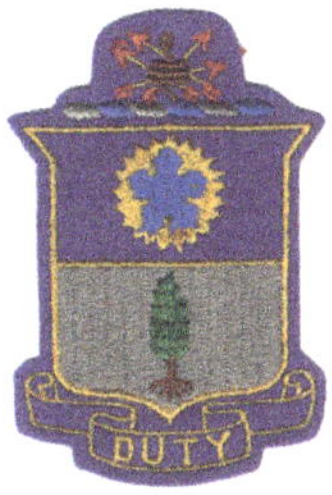
DUTY
21st Inf. Regt.

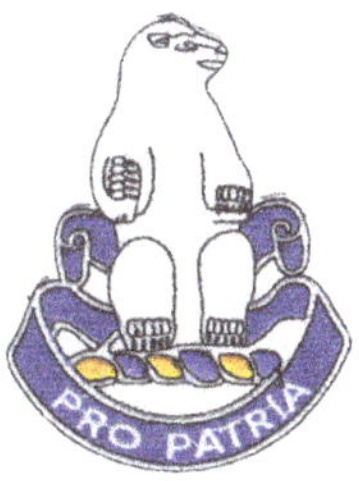
PRO PATRIA
31st Inf. Regt.

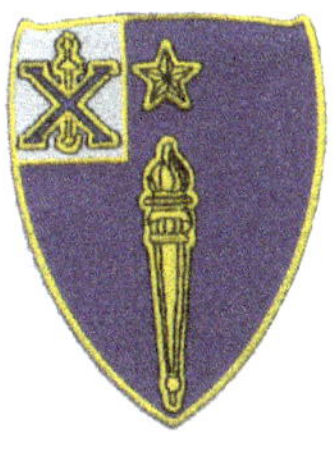
46th Inf. Regt.

198th Infantry Brigade "Brave and Bold"

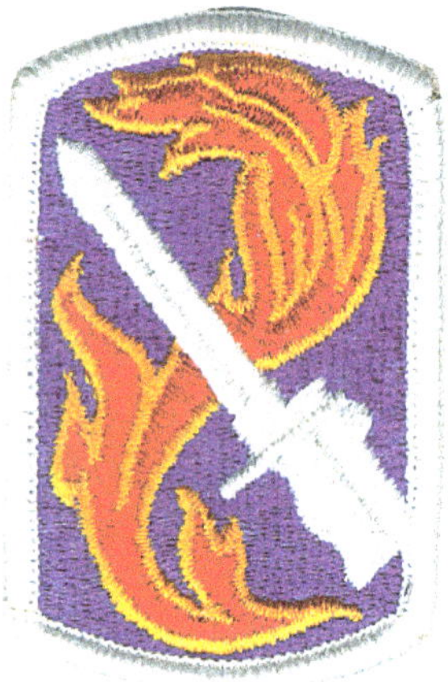

Landed in RVN: 21 Oct. 1967
Left RVN: 17 Nov. 1971
Locale: Duc Pho, Chu Lai

Shoulder Sleeve Insignia

On a blue shield arched at top and base 3 inches in height and 2 inches in width overall a stylized tongue of flame *(shaped like an "S" reversed)* yellow and scarlet with a portion of a rifle barrel with fixed bayonet all in white issuing diagonally from lower right to upper left and crossing over the flame all with a $^{1}/_{8}$ inch white border.

Blue and white are the colors used for Infantry. The tongue of flame alludes to the unit's fire power and the bayonet, a basic Infantry weapon, is symbolic of carrying the fight to the enemy. The flame and bayonet together thus refer to the unit's spirit and readiness to engage the enemy in fire fight or in hand-to-hand combat with the bayonet. The shoulder sleeve insignia was approved on 6 July 1967.

Distinctive Unit Insignia

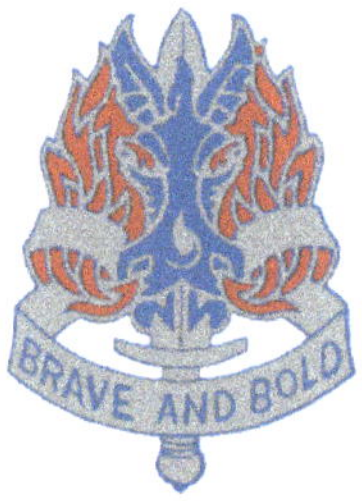
BRAVE AND BOLD

Distinctive Unit Insignia

A device of silver color metal and enamel 1 $^{1}/_{4}$ inches in height overall consisting of a blue dragon's head facing front with red eyes and nostrils, the last emitting red and orange flames upward along each side; entering the animal's mouth in base the blade of a silver sword with point emerging above between the ears. On either side, entwining the flames and curving across the hilt of the sword a silver scroll bearing the motto *"BRAVE AND BOLD"* in blue letters.

The great strength and terrible weapons of the mythical dragon are synonymous with the enemies the Brigade may face and the sword impaling his head denotes the fighting spirit displayed in the face of great odds and the victorious results. Underneath, the unit's motto *"BRAVE AND BOLD"* describes the basic qualities of the men of the 198th Infantry. The distinctive unit insignia was approved on 20 October 1967.

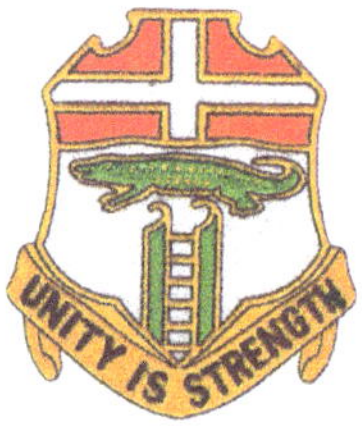
UNITY IS STRENGTH

6th Inf. Regt.

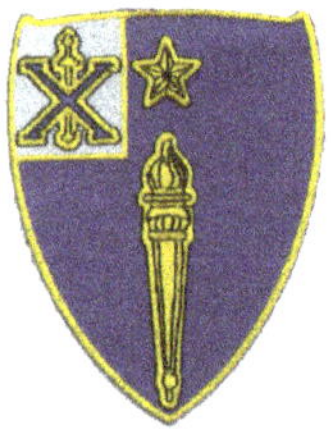

46th Inf. Regt.

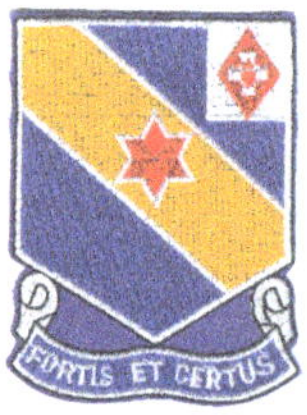
FORTIS ET CERTUS

52nd Inf. Regt.

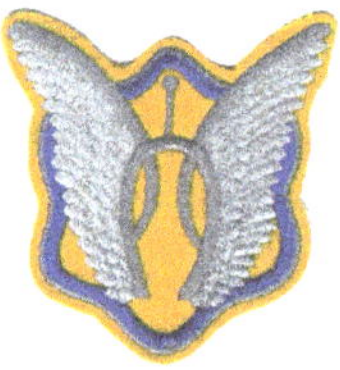

17th Cavalry Regt.

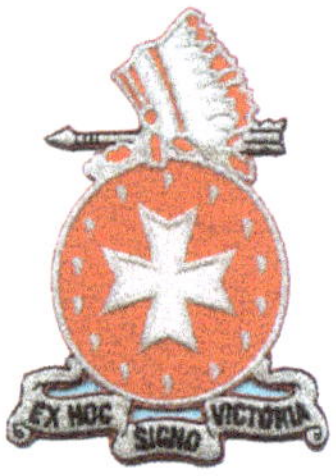
EX HOC SIGNO VICTORIA

14th Fld. Arty. Regt.

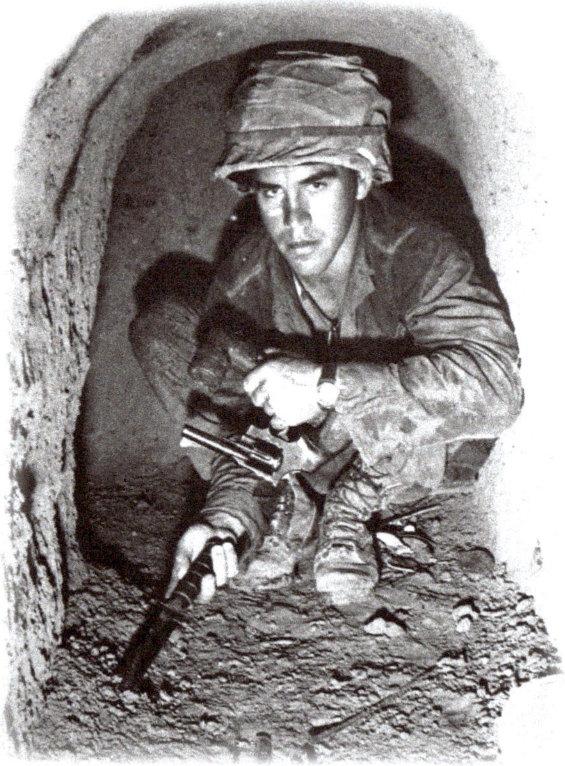

199th Infantry Brigade “The Redcatchers”

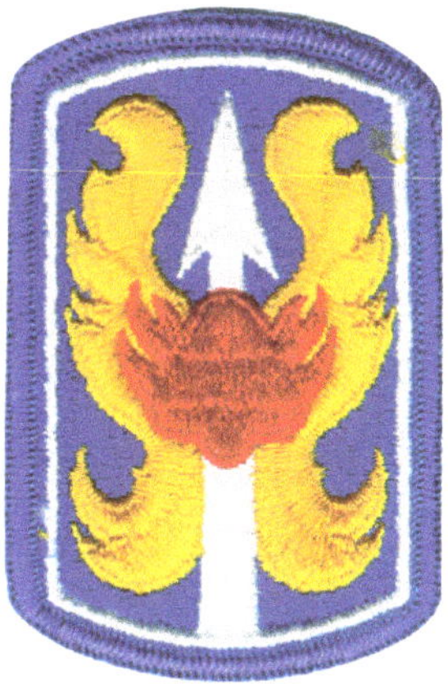

Shoulder Sleeve Insignia

On a shield, oblong in shape and arched at both ends, 3 inches (7.62 cm) in height and 2 inches (5.08 cm) in width overall, edged with a $^1/_8$ inch (.32 cm) blue border fimbriated by a $^1/_{16}$ inch (.16 cm) white inner edge on a blue background, the upper length of a white spear, the area below the spearhead enveloped with a stylized yellow flame having an inner core of red.

The colors blue and white are used for Infantry. The spear, an early Infantry weapon in flames, symbolizes the evolution and firepower of the modern Infantry.

The shoulder sleeve insignia was approved on 10 June 1966.

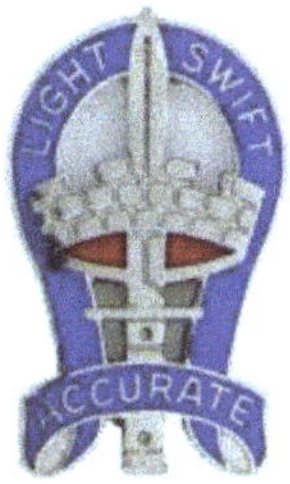
LIGHT SWIFT
ACCURATE

Distinctive Unit Insignia

Distinctive Unit Insignia

A silver color metal and enamel device 1 $^1/_4$ inches (3.18 cm) in height consisting of a vertical silver bayonet, the blade encircled by a silver mural crown lined with red *(scarlet)* all within a stylized continuous scroll in blue *(Infantry blue)*, the scroll passing under the point of the bayonet and over the bayonet handle and partially behind the crown and bayonet guard, and bearing at top the two words "LIGHT" "SWIFT" and at base the word "ACCURATE" all in silver letters.

Landed in RVN: 10 Dec. 1966
Left RVN: 11 Oct. 1970
Locale: Song Be, Bien Hoa, Long Binh

Symbolism

The light blue refers to Infantry and the red to Artillery elements of the organization. The bayonet, a basic weapon of Infantry élan, refers to Fort Benning *(The Infantry School)* where the organization was activated while the mural crown alludes to the Infantry sobriquet "Queen of Battles." The mural crown is also heraldically symbolic of aggressive and successful attack on a fortified position or beleagured city and in ancient times was given as a sign of courage and triumph to the unit which first stormed and scaled a city's walls. The three words of the motto allude to the organization's mobility and accuracy of fire and operation in the accomplishment of its mission. The distinctive unit insignia was approved on 27 June 1966.

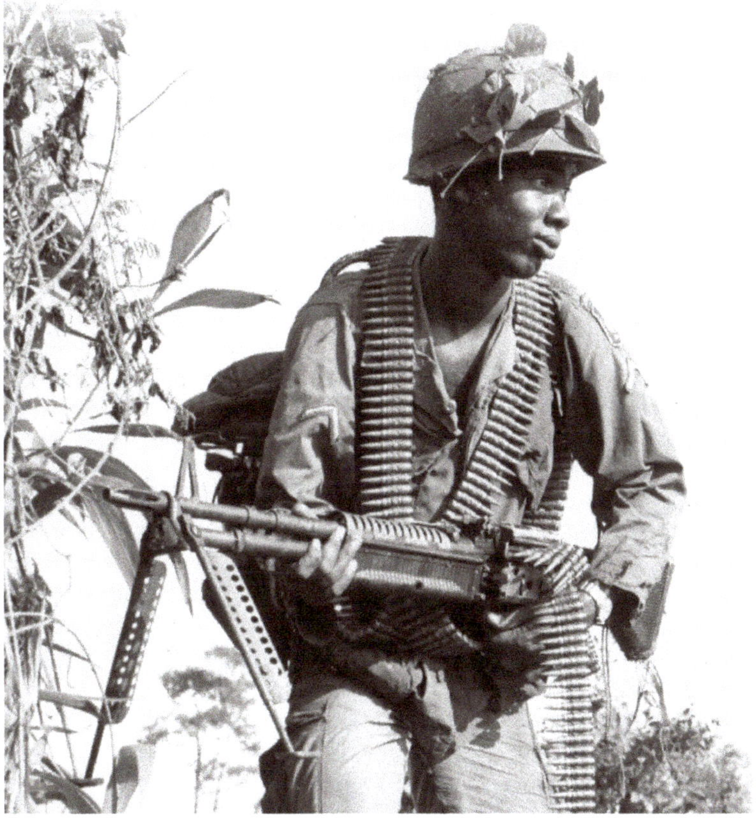

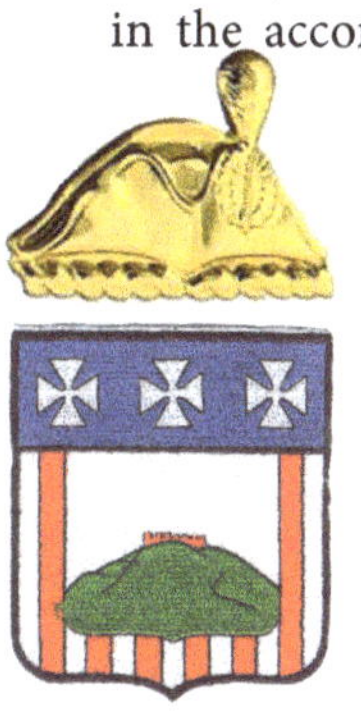

3rd Inf. Regt.

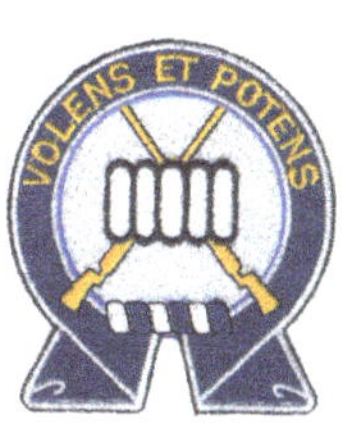
VOLENS ET POTENS

7th Inf. Regt.

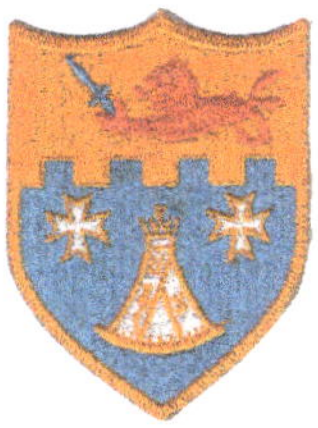

12th Inf. Regt.

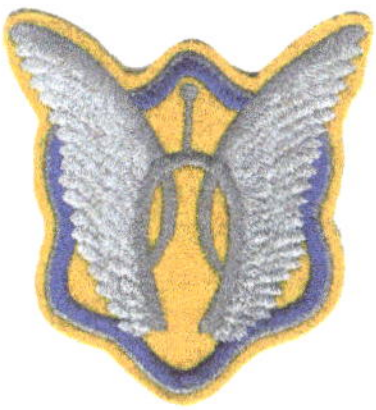

17th Cavalry Regt.

5th Special Forces Group (Airborne) "The Legion Legionnaires"

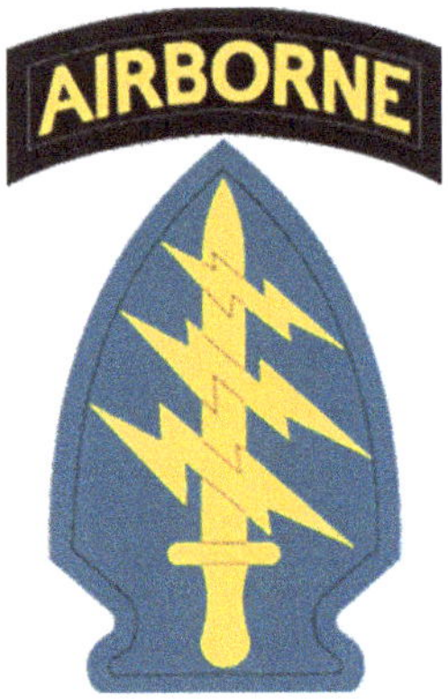
AIRBORNE

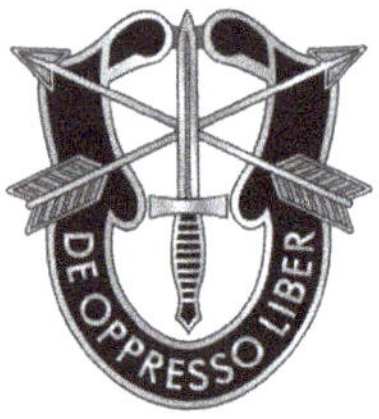
DE OPPRESSO LIBER

Distinctive Unit Insignia

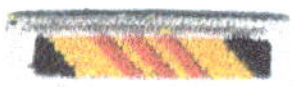

TAB

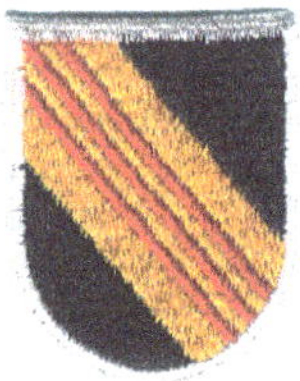

5th S. F. Group In Vietnam

Landed in RVN: 1 Oct. 1964
Left RVN: 3 March 1971
Locale: South Vietnam

Shoulder Sleeve Insignia

On a teal blue arrowhead $3\,^{1}/_{8}$ inches in height and 2 inches in width, point up, a yellow dagger, its blade surmounted by three yellow lightning flashes, bendwise in pale, all inset $^{1}/_{8}$ inch from the edge of the arrowhead. On a tab placed $^{3}/_{16}$ inch above the insignia, the word *"AIRBORNE"* in yellow letters on a black background.

Symbolism

The arrowhead alludes to the American Indian's basic skills in which Special Forces personnel are trained to a high degree. The dagger represents the unconventional nature of Special Forces operations, and the three lightning flashes, their ability to strike rapidly by air, water or land.

The shoulder sleeve insignia was originally approved on 22 August 1955. It was amended to add an airborne tab on 20 November 1958. The insignia was authorized to be worn by personnel of the U.S. Army Special Forces Command *(Airborne)* and its subordinate units not authorized a shoulder sleeve insignia in their own right on 7 March 1991. The wear of the insignia by the U.S. Army Special Forces Command *(Airborne)* and its subordinate units was cancelled and it was authorized to be worn by personnel of the 1st Special Forces Command *(Airborne)* and their subordinate units not authorized a shoulder sleeve insignia in their own right on 27 October 2016.

Distinctive Unit Insignia

A silver color metal and enamel device $1\,^{1}/_{8}$ inches in height consisting of a pair of silver arrows in saltire, points up and surmounted at their junction by a silver dagger with black handle point up; all over and between a black motto scroll arcing to base and inscribed *"DE OPPRESSO LIBER"* in silver letters.

Symbolism

The insignia is the crossed arrow collar insignia *(insignia of branch)* of the First Special Force, World War II combined with the fighting knife which is of a distinctive shape and pattern only issued to the First Special Service Force. The motto is translated as *"From Oppression We Will Liberate Them."* The distinctive unit insignia was approved on 8 July 1960.

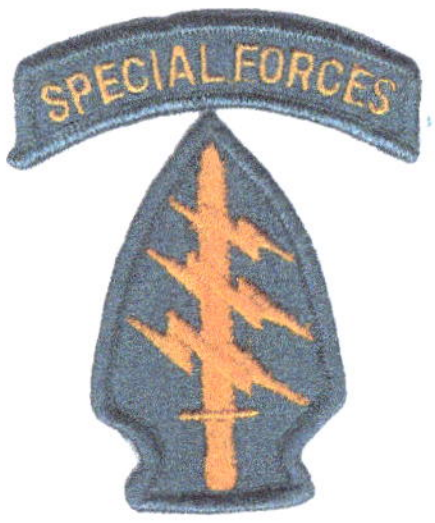
SPECIAL FORCES

Special Forces

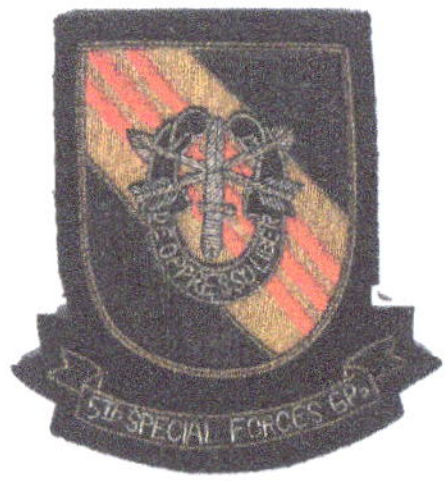

5th Special Fces. Grp.

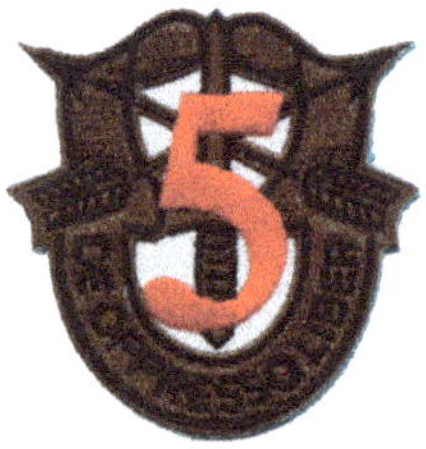
5

5th Special Fces. Grp.

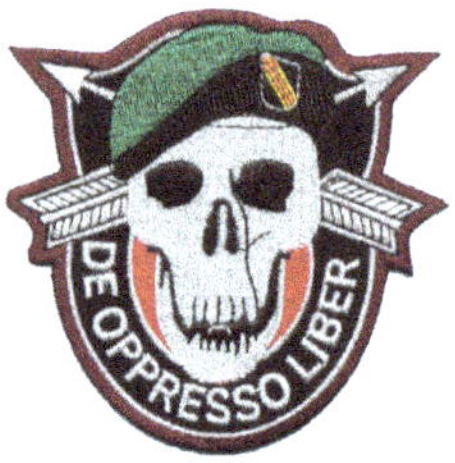
DE OPPRESSO LIBER

5th S.F.G. Black Ops.

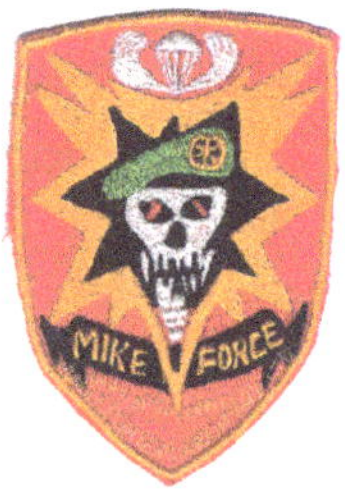
MIKE FORCE

C - 1 Mike Force

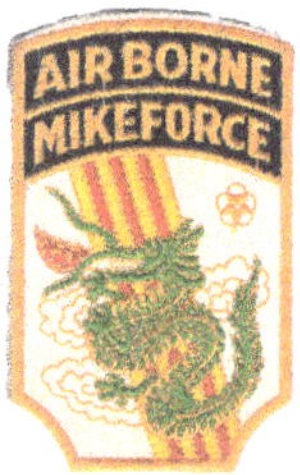
AIRBORNE
MIKEFORCE

C - 4 Mike Force

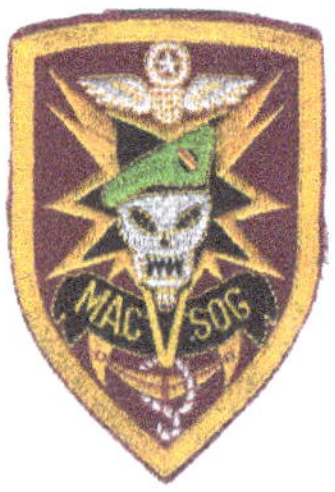
MAC SOG

MAC-V SOG

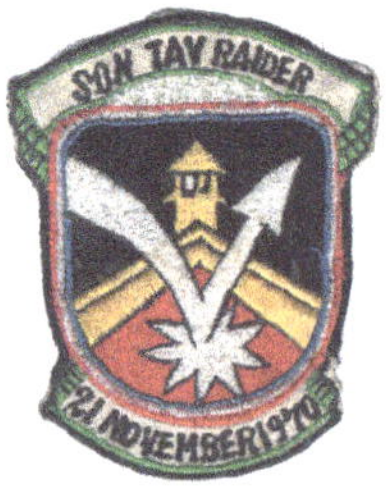
SON TAY RAIDER

Son Tay Raid

1st Squadron, 1st Cavalry Regiment "1st Regiment of Dragoons"

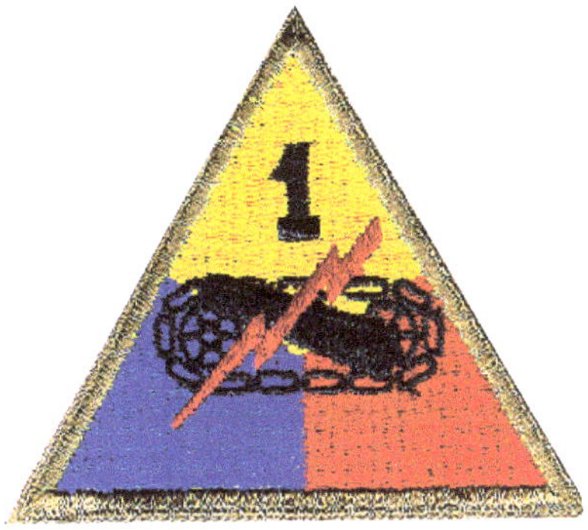
1

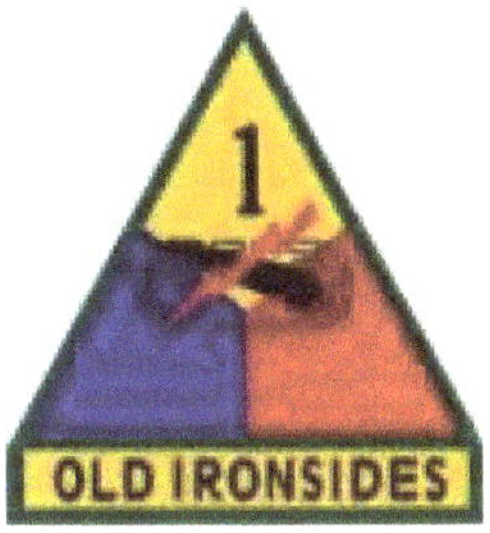
1
OLD IRONSIDES

Shoulder Sleeve Insignia

An equilateral triangle, one point up, above a horizontal tab attached in base, the overall dimensions of triangle and tab is $4\ ^{1}/_{16}$ inches in height and $3\ ^{7}/_{8}$ inches in width, the triangle is divided into three sections, the upper section yellow, the left section blue and the right section red.

There is a cannon in front of a tank track and wheels surmounted by a red lightning flash bend sinister wise. In the apex the Arabic numeral "1" in black, all within a $^{1}/_{8}$ inch green border. When worn with the yellow tab the inscription *"OLD IRONSIDES"* in black letters $^{5}/_{16}$ inch in height.

Yellow, blue, and red are the colors of the branches from which armored units were formed. The tank tread, gun, and lightning flash are symbolic of mobility, power, and speed. The Division's designation is in Arabic numerals. The shoulder sleeve insignia was originally approved without the tab on 22 November 1940. The tab was authorized as a separate item on 21 February 1956. The insignia was changed to a one-piece insignia on 5 November 1970.

Arriving in Vietnam in August, 1967, the Squadron consisted of three Armored Cavalry Troops and one Air Cavalry Troop, D Troop, which was not deployed until July 1968. The Squadron immediately deployed in the I Corps Tactical Zone around the city of Chu Lai. It was committed to battle two days after its arrival, operating against the North Vietnamese Army and Vietcong. From 1 September 1967 to June 1968, the Squadron was involved in eleven major battles and numerous smaller engagements; among these were Cigar Island, Que Son Valley, Pineapple Forest, the Western Valley and Tam Ky. The Air Cavalry Troop, Troop D, joined the Squadron 21 July 1968, disembarking at Da Nang and flew directly to Camp Eagle. The Troop remained on combat duty in I CORP for the next four years using the call sign Sabre.

In the Pineapple Forest Battle of February 1968, the ground-air cavalry team had its greatest victory, killing 180 of the enemy without losing one of its own number. 1st Squadron, 1st Cavalry Regiment remained in the field continuously during the Vietnam War from 1967-1972, attached as an independent Squadron to elements of the 101st Airborne Division and took part in 13 campaigns. The Squadron departed Vietnam on 10 May 1972.

Landed in RVN: 29 Aug. 1967:
Left RVN: 10 May 1972
Locale: Chu Lai, Da Nang, Tam Ky

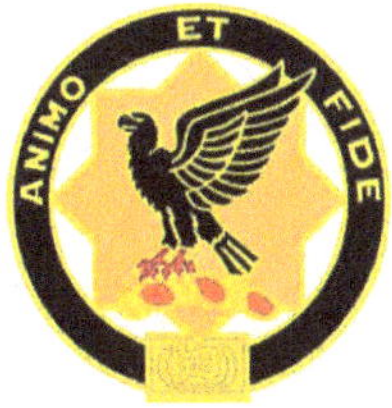
ANIMO
ET
FIDE

Distinctive Unit Insignia

Distinctive Unit Insignia

On a heraldic wreath gold and Dragoon Yellow is a hawk rising with wings elevated upon an eight-pointed Dragoon Yellow star surrounded by a Black sword belt bearing the organizational motto *"ANIMO ET FIDE"* (*"Courageous and Faithful"*) from the old Dragoon belt plate of 1836. The insignia is $1\ ^{1}/_{4}$ inches in diameter.

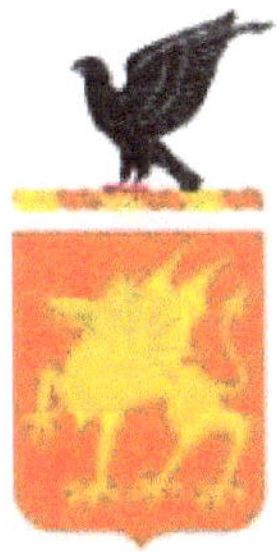

Coat of Arms

Symbolism

This Regiment was organized in 1833 as the Regiment of United States Dragoons. Many of its officers and men came from the Battalion of Mounted Rangers which had taken part in the Black Hawk War. The color of the Dragoons was Dragoon yellow *(orange-yellow)* and a gold eight-pointed star on the encircling belt was the insignia of the Dragoons until 1851. The motto translates to *"Courageous and Faithful."* The distinctive unit insignia was originally approved for the 1st Cavalry Regiment on 27 November 1923. It was redesignated for the 1st Armored Regiment on 7 September 1940. It was redesignated for the 1st Constabulary Squadron on 11 June 1947. The insignia was redesignated for the 1st Medium Tank Battalion on 13 August 1951. It was redesignated for the 1st Tank Battalion on 18 February 1955. The insignia was redesignated for the 1st Cavalry Regiment on 21 April 1958. It was amended to change the wording of the description on 20 October 1965.

2nd Squadron, 1st Cavalry "1st Regiment of Dragoons"

Landed in RVN: 30 Aug. 1967
Left RVN: 10 Oct. 1970
Locale: Pleiku, Dak To, Song Mao

Shoulder Sleeve Insignia

An equilateral triangle, one point up, above a horizontal tab attached in base, the overall dimensions of triangle and tab 4 1/16 inches in height and 3 7/8 inches in width, the triangle divided into three sections, the upper section yellow, the left section blue and the right section red, a gun lies across in front of a tank track and wheels surmounted by a red lightning flash. In the apex the Arabic numeral "2" in black, all within a 1/8 inch green border. When worn with the tab the inscription *"HELL ON WHEELS"* is in black letters 5/16 inch in height.

Yellow, blue and red are the colors of the branches from which armored units were formed. The tank tread, gun and lightning flash are symbolic of mobility, power and speed. The division's designation is in an Arabic numeral. The shoulder sleeve insignia was originally approved on 22 November 1940. It was amended for the addition of a tab on 16 August 1954. The insignia was further amended to revise the design to make the insignia and tab in one piece on 4 November 1970.

On 8 August 1967, the unit left Fort Hood for Vietnam where they were attached to the 4th Infantry Division, headquartered in Pleiku. During their service in the Central Highlands, troopers saw action in Pleiku, Dak To, Suoi Doi, Kon Tum, An Khe and many other nameless stretches of road and jungle. In May 1969, the squadron was transferred to Task Force South in Phan Thiết and was attached to the 1st Field Force, Vietnam. Operating in the rice paddies and rubber plantations of Vietnam, the Blackhawks further distinguished themselves in actions around Phan Thiết, Song Mao, Phan Rang and their environs. 2-1 Cavalry departed Vietnam in October 1970, leaving Cam Ranh Bay for reassignment to the 2nd Armored Division at Fort Hood, Texas.

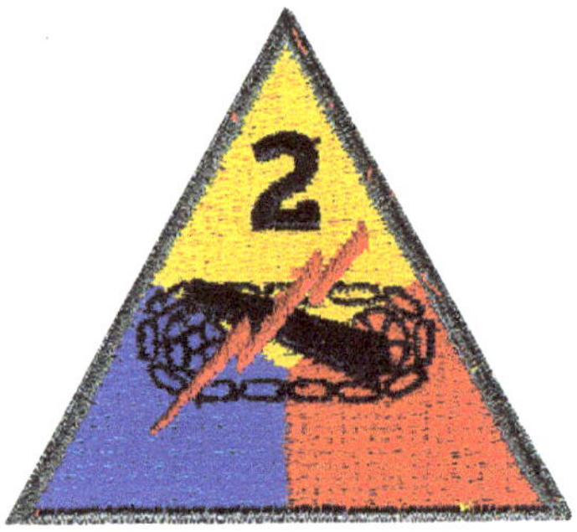
2

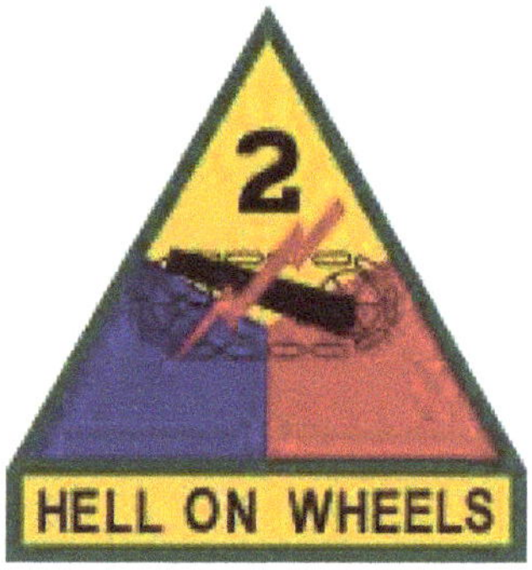
2
HELL ON WHEELS

Distinctive Unit Insignia

On a heraldic wreath Or and Tenné *(Dragoon Yellow)* a hawk rising with wings addorsed and elevated Sable and membered Gules-charged upon an eight-pointed Dragoon Yellow star surrounded by a Black sword belt bearing the organizational motto *"ANIMO ET FIDE"* with the old Dragoon belt plate of 1836. The insignia is 1 1/4 inches in diameter. This Regiment was organized in 1833 as the Regiment of United States Dragoons. Many of its officers and men came from the Battalion of Mounted Rangers which had taken part in the Black Hawk War. The color of the Dragoons was Dragoon yellow *(orange-yellow)* and a gold eight-pointed star on the encircling belt was the insignia of the Dragoons until 1851. The motto translates to *"Courageous and Faithful."* The distinctive unit insignia was originally approved for the 1st Cavalry Regiment on 27 November 1923. It was redesignated for the 1st Armored Regiment on 7 September 1940. It was redesignated for the 1st Constabulary Squadron on 11 June 1947. The insignia was redesignated for the 1st Medium Tank Battalion on 13 August 1951. It was redesignated for the 1st Tank Battalion on 18 February 1955. The insignia was redesignated for the 1st Cavalry Regiment on 21 April 1958. It was amended to change the wording of the description on 20 October 1965.

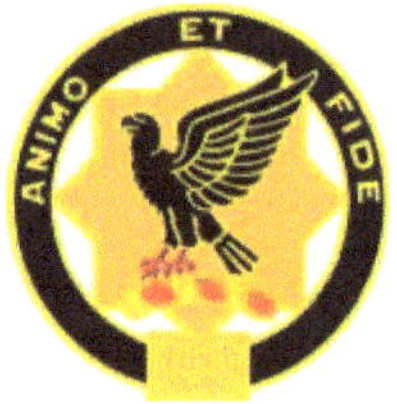
ANIMO ET FIDE

Distinctive Unit Insignia

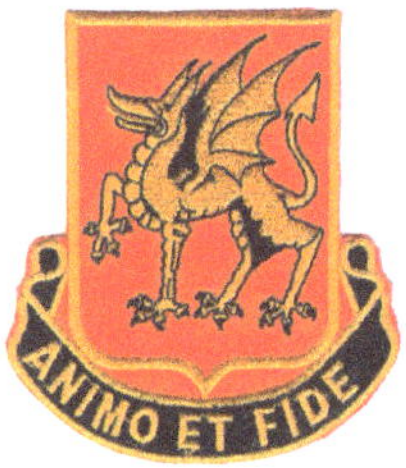
ANIMO ET FIDE

1st Cav. Regt.

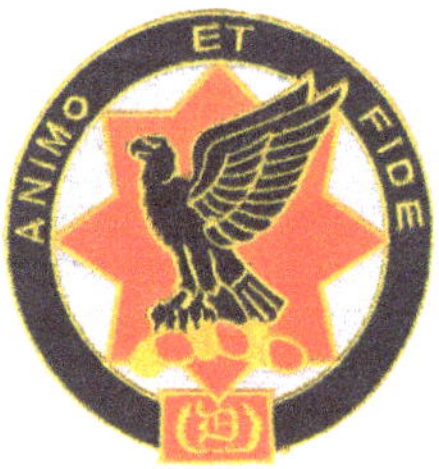
ANIMO ET FIDE

1st Cav. Regt.

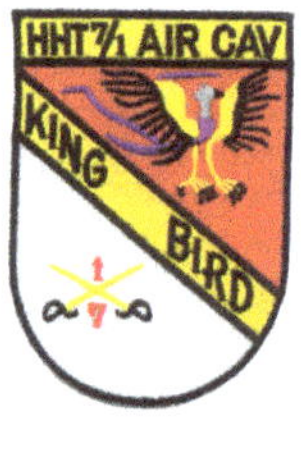
HHT 7/1 AIR CAV
KING BIRD

1st Air. Cav.
7th Sqdn-HHT

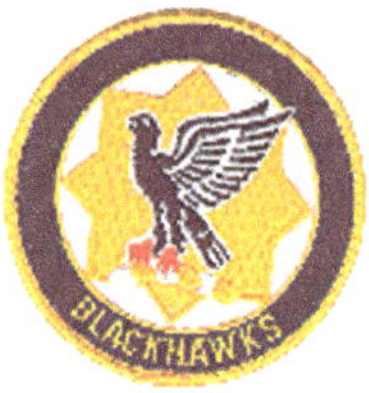
BLACKHAWKS

1st Cav. Regt.
7th Squadron

U.S. Army Criminal Investigation Command

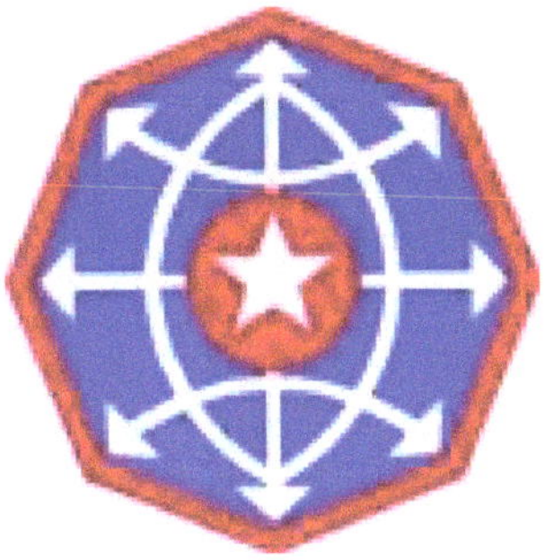

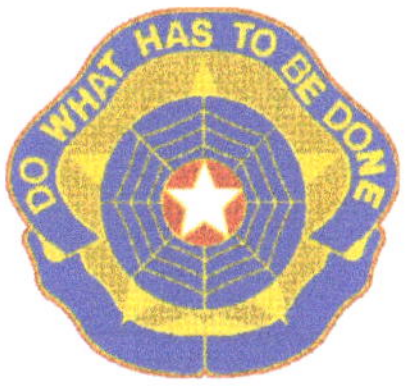
DO WHAT HAS TO BE DONE

Distinctive Unit Insignia

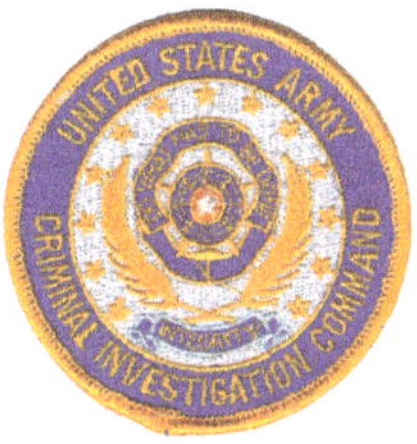
UNITED STATES ARMY
CRIMINAL INVESTIGATION COMMAND

Criminal Invest. Command

Shoulder Sleeve Insignia

On a blue octagon $2\ ^{1}/_{2}$ inches in diameter and within a $^{1}/_{8}$ inch red border, the latitude and longitude lines of a global map terminating in arrowheads within the angles of the border all in white, and at center on a red disc a white five-pointed star.

The central star and the lines of the latitude and longitude suggesting a globe, together with the arrowheads marking the points of a compass, symbolize the basic mission of the Command: to perform and exercise centralized command, authority, direction and control of Army criminal investigation activities worldwide. Blue, white and red are the national colors. The shoulder sleeve insignia was authorized for the US Army Criminal Investigation Command on 12 Nov 1971.

Distinctive Unit Insignia

A gold color metal and enamel device $1\ ^{3}/_{16}$ inches in height overall consisting of a gold five-pointed star with points protruding beyond the rim of a surmounted blue enamel disc bearing gold grid lines throughout simulating a web, overall in center a scarlet disc charged with a white enamel five-pointed star throughout, all enclosed by a wavy blue enamel scroll folded back on each side and terminating at base and inscribed at the top *"DO WHAT HAS TO BE DONE"* in gold letters.

Landed in RVN: 1968
Left RVN: 1972
Locale: Long Binh

The central star symbolizes centralized command. The grid lines allude to the latitude and longitude lines of the globe thus referring to the worldwide activities of the organization. The grid lines also suggest a stylized web, with the eight sides representing the eight geographical regions of the Command. The web, a symbol of criminal apprehension, is the result of methodical construction thus alluding to the scientific methods of criminal investigation. The outer points of the star further symbolize far-reaching authority. Blue, white and red are the national colors and gold is symbolic of achievement. The distinctive unit insignia was approved for the US Army Criminal Investigation Command on 6 Jun 1972.

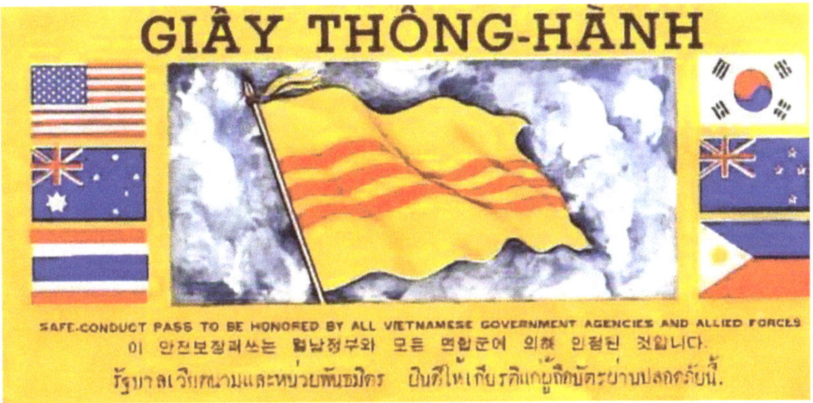
GIẤY THÔNG-HÀNH
SAFE-CONDUCT PASS TO BE HONORED BY ALL VIETNAMESE GOVERNMENT AGENCIES AND ALLIED FORCES

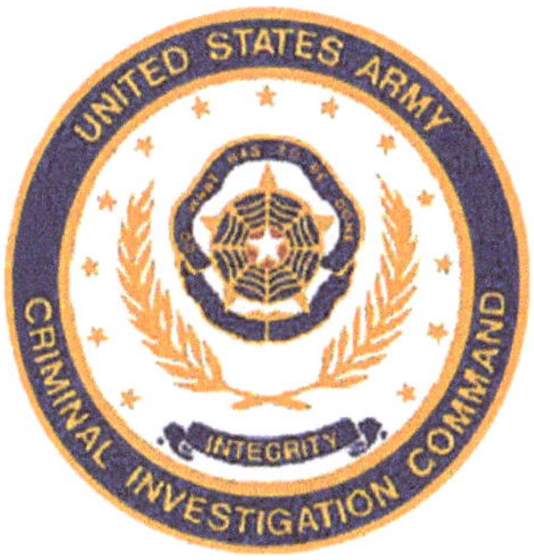
UNITED STATES ARMY
CRIMINAL INVESTIGATION COMMAND
INTEGRITY

U.S. Army Criminal Investigation Division Seal

US Army Security Agency Group, Vietnam

Landed in RVN: 25 May 1961
Left RVN:7 March 1973
Locale: Saigon

Shoulder Sleeve Insignia

A shield framed in gold with the talon of an eagle grasping two white lightening bolts. The patch symbolizes the ability to intercept enemy communications.

ASA personnel of the 3rd Radio Research Unit were covertly designated as Radio Research and were among the earliest U.S. military personnel in Vietnam. The 3rd later expanded to become the 509th Radio Research Group.

Most ASA personnel processed *"in country"* through Davis Station. Others attached to larger command structures prior to transport to Vietnam processed in with those units. ASA personnel were attached to Army infantry and armored cavalry units throughout the Vietnam War. Some teams were also attached to the Studies and Observation Group of Military Assistance Command Vietnam and special forces units. Assigned to the 5th Special Forces Group *(Airborne)* based out of Nha Trang was the 403rd Radio Research Group, Special Operations Detachment *(SOD)*. SOD forces were deployed to Operational Detachment base camps throughout South Vietnam. Other teams, such as the 313th Radio Research Battalion at Nha Trang, were independent of other Army units. ASA personnel were kept in Vietnam after the 1973 pullout of US Army combat forces; they were finally withdrawn with other US personnel at the fall of Saigon in April 1975.

Distinctive Unit Insignia

VIGILANT
ALWAYS

Distinctive Unit Insignia

A gold, green and black color metal and enamel device 1 $^{3}/_{16}$ inches in height overall consisting of a globe in the center with symbols representing communication intercept enclosed by two gold scrolls inscribed *"Vigilant Always"*.

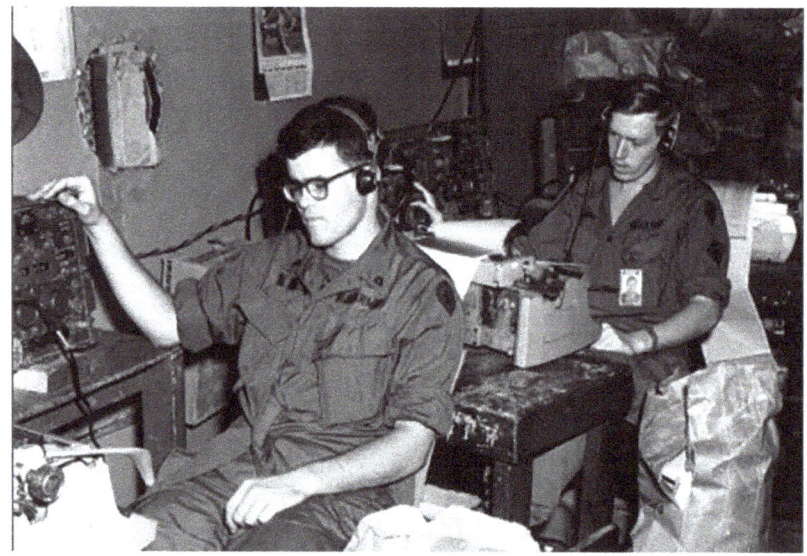

335TH
RADIO RESEARCH
CMA

335th Radio Research Unit Station

224th MI BN (AE)
GUARDRAIL

VIGILANCE ABOVE

224th M. I. Bn.

SAVOIR C'EST POUVOIR

313th M. I. Bn.

313th ASA Bn. - Nha Trang

1st Aviation Brigade "Gunfighters"

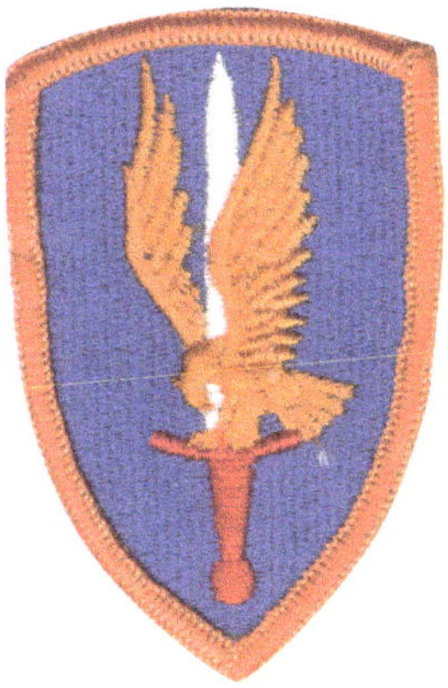

Shoulder Sleeve Insignia

On a blue *(ultramarine)* shield arched at top $2\,^1/_4$ inches in width a golden orange swooping hawk head to left and wings elevated in front of a vertical unsheathed sword, point upward throughout with white blade and red hilt all within a golden orange $^1/_8$ inch border.

Landed in RVN: 25 May 1966
Left RVN: 28 March 1973
Locale: Vietnam

Symbolism

Blue and golden orange are the colors of Army Aviation. The gold of the hawk and the red of the sword handle are the colors of the Republic of Vietnam, and of the shoulder sleeve insignia of the U.S. Military Assistance Command, Vietnam and U.S. Army, Vietnam, the Commands under which the Aviation Brigade was formed and under which it first served in armed conflict. The hawk in flight preparing to strike its prey is symbolic of Army Aviation's impact on modern ground warfare. The hawk was adopted as the symbol of the new capabilities of Army Aviation during the initial phase of Air Assault concept testing in 1963. The crusader's sword is taken from the shoulder sleeve insignia of the U.S. Military Assistance Command, Vietnam and identifies the origin and mission of the Aviation Brigade in Vietnam. The rapid and quantum increase in the Army Aviation units in Vietnam dictated formation of an Aviation Brigade for command of multiple battalions of Army Aviation organizations. The shoulder sleeve insignia was approved on 2 August 1966.

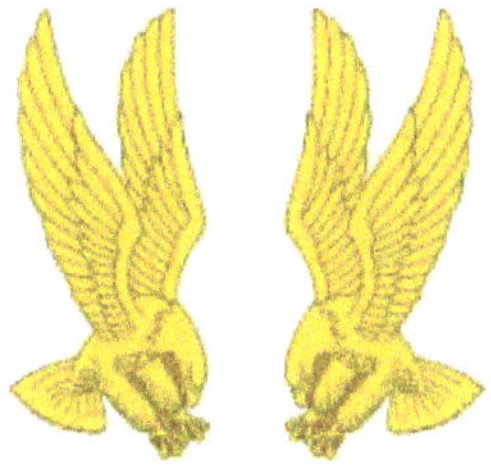

Distinctive Unit Insignia

Distinctive Unit Insignia

A gold colored metal device $1\,^3/_8$ inches in height consisting of a swooping hawk with elevated wings, head to left for wear on the left shoulder, and head to right for wear on right shoulder, with detail in black.

Symbolism

Gold is one of the colors of the Republic of Vietnam, and of the shoulder sleeve insignia of the U.S. Military Assistance Command, Vietnam and U.S. Army, Vietnam, the Commands under which the Brigade was formed and served in armed conflict. The hawk in flight preparing to strike its prey symbolizes aviation's impact on modern ground warfare.

The distinctive unit insignia was approved on 2 August 1966. *See next page for displays.*

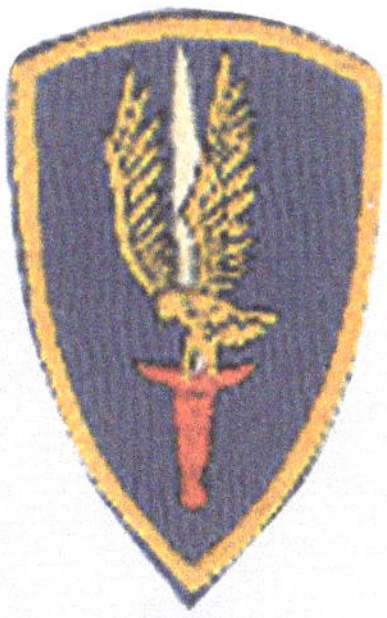

1st Avn. Brigade

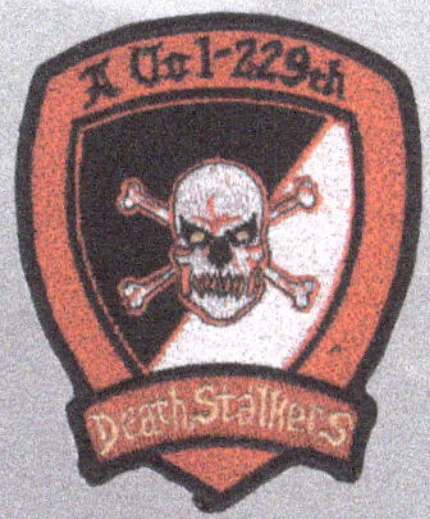
A Co 1-229th
Death Stalkers

229th Avn. Regt. 1st Bn. - A Co.

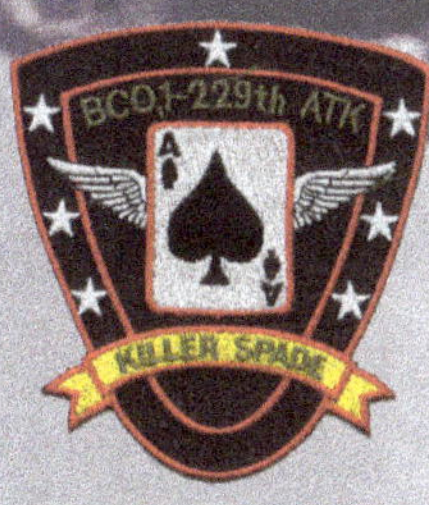
BCO 1-229th ATK
KILLER SPADE

229th Avn. Regt. 1st Bn. - B Co.

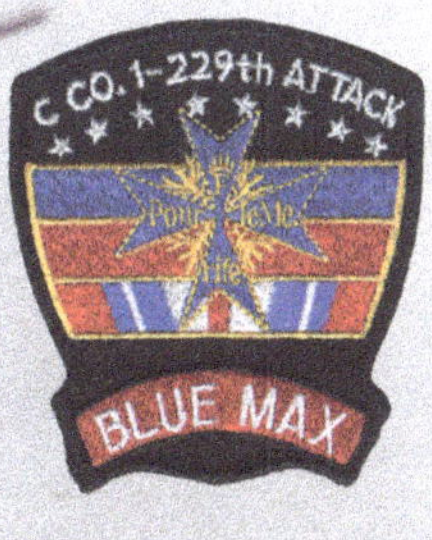
C CO. 1-229th ATTACK
BLUE MAX

229th Atk. Helic.Regt. - 1st Bn. - C Co.

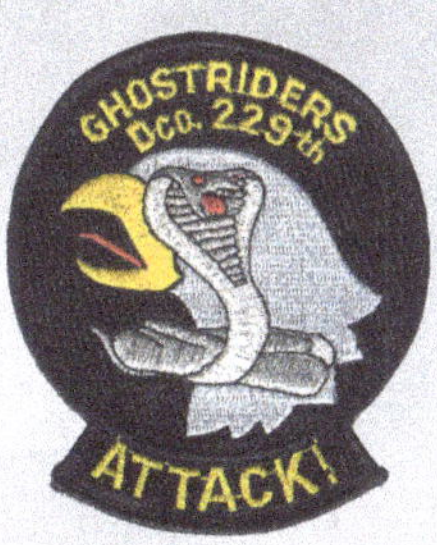
GHOSTRIDERS
Dco. 229th
ATTACK!

229th Avn. Regt. 1st Bn. - D Co.

1st Aviation Brigade "Gunfighters"

Engineer Command, Vietnam

No Distinctive Unit Insignia

Landed in RVN: 1 Dec. 1966
Left RVN: 30 April 1972
Located: Long Binh

Shoulder Sleeve Insignia

A shield 3 inches in height and 2 inches in width consisting of a $1/8$ inch white border around a scarlet field charged at center with a white hexagonal fortress with six turrets surmounted by two vertical crusaders' swords their points to top with white blades and yellow hilts.

The shield shape is similar to those of the Military Assistance Command, Vietnam and the United States Army, Vietnam, symbolizing the Engineer Command's common interest and joint efforts with these headquarters. The colors, scarlet and white, refer to the Corps of Engineers, while scarlet and yellow are the colors of the flag of the Republic of Vietnam. The three colors combined (scarlet, white and yellow) represent the Engineer Command's commitments in combat engineering, construction and facilities engineering services throughout the entire Republic of Vietnam. The two crusaders' swords symbolize the roles of the Engineer Command with its two major military arms, the 18th and 20th Engineer Brigades, in military assistance and defense of the Republic of Vietnam. The hexagonal figure is a fortress viewed from above and represents a fortification traditionally associated with military engineering through the ages. The upper three turrets of the fortress represent the three Engineer Groups of the 18th Engineer Brigade which operated in the upper half of the Republic of Vietnam, and the lower three turrets the three Engineer Groups of the 20th Engineer Brigade whose area of operations was the lower half of the Republic of Vietnam. The division of the fortress into three elements by the superimposed swords refers to the three Engineer Districts into which the Command area of responsibility is divided for Facilities Engineering.

The shoulder sleeve insignia was approved on 2 February 1971. It was cancelled effective 30 April 1972.

36 Shoulder Sleeve Insignia and Crest of the U.S. Army Vietnam

18th Engineer Brigade “Let Us Try and Let Us Build”

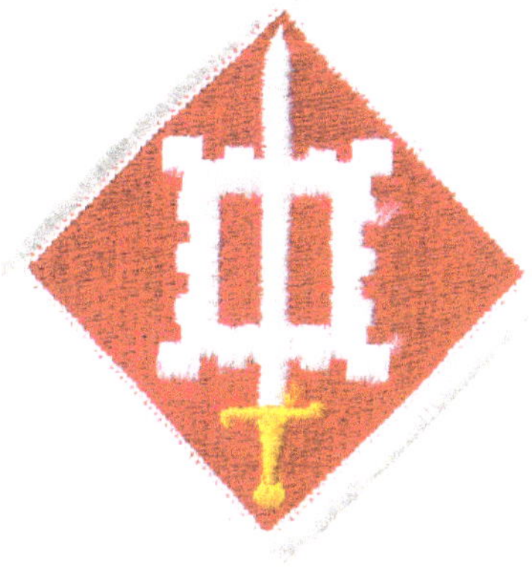

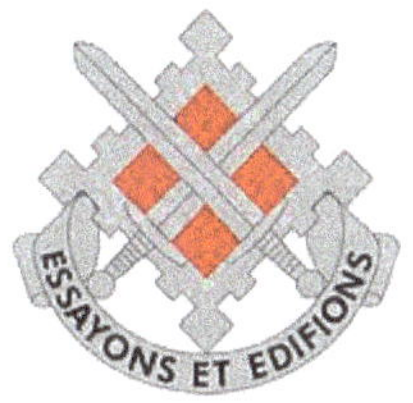
ESSAYONS ET EDIFIONS
Distinctive Unit Insignia

Shoulder Sleeve Insignia

On a red square, one point up, 2 $^{1}/_{2}$ inches in height and 2 $^{1}/_{2}$ inches in width a white stylized fortress, embattled on its outer edges and voided of the field, surmounted by a vertical white sword, point up and hilted yellow, all within a white 1/8 inch border.

Scarlet and white are the colors used for the Engineers. The four corners of the crenelated square allude to their four campaigns in World War II: Normandy, Northern France, Rhineland and Central Europe. The four sides of the central red square stand for planning, training, construction and combat support. The sword symbolizes preparedness in peace and unrelenting fulfillment of Engineer missions in time of war. The white outer border symbolizes unit integrity.

The shoulder sleeve insignia was approved on 10 February 1966.

Distinctive Unit Insignia

A silver color metal and enamel device 1 $^{1}/_{8}$ inches overall, consisting of a four bastion fort one point down silver, the interior in red. On top of this is placed two crossed swords saltirewise in silver. Under the design is a silver motto scroll bearing the legend *"ESSAYONS ET EDIFIONS"* in black.

Landed in RVN: 20 Sept 1965
Left RVN: 20 Sept. 1971
Locale: Tan Son Nhut, Bong Ba Thin

Scarlet and white *(silver)* are the colors used for the Engineers. The four sides of the fort stand for planning, training, construction and combat support. The crenelations of the fort represent the Brigade's participation in campaigns of World War II: Normandy, Northern France, Rhineland and Central Europe. The crossed swords symbolize preparedness in peace, and unrelenting fulfillment of Engineer missions in time of war. The motto "Essayons et Edifions" emblazoned on the scroll is translated as *"Let Us Try and Let Us Build."*

The distinctive unit insignia was approved on 3 August 1966. On 20 September 1971 the Brigade was inactivated. Over the six years that it served in Vietnam, the 18th Engineer Brigade was involved in 14 of 17 campaigns, earning four Meritorious Unit Commendations.

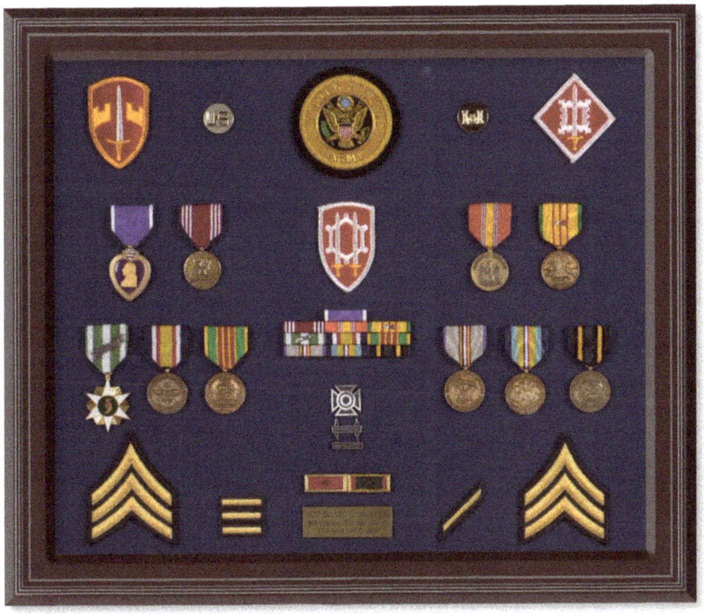

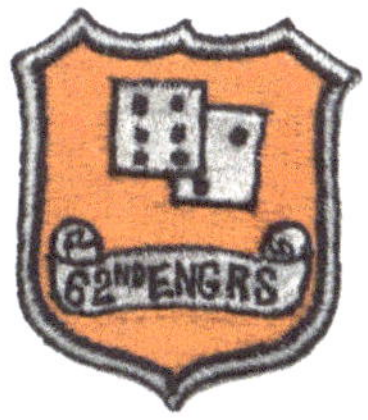
62ND ENGRS
62Nd Engineers

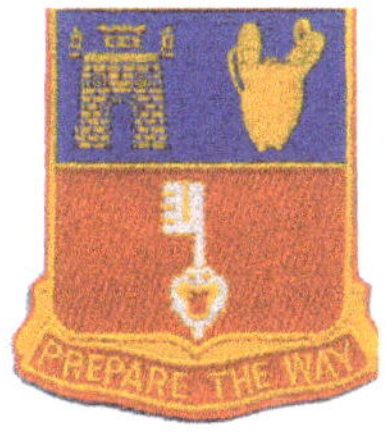
PREPARE THE WAY
116th Engr.Bn.

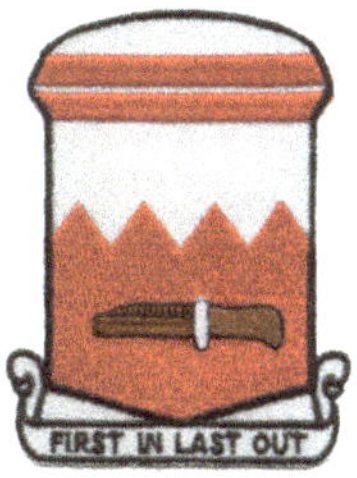
FIRST IN LAST OUT
65th Engr. Bn.

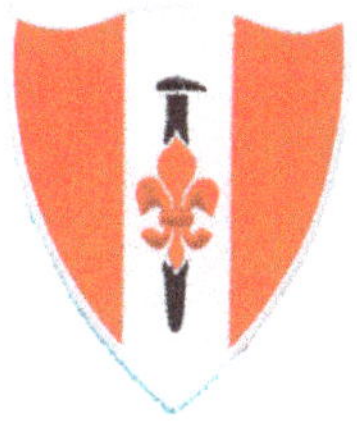
46th Engr.Bn.

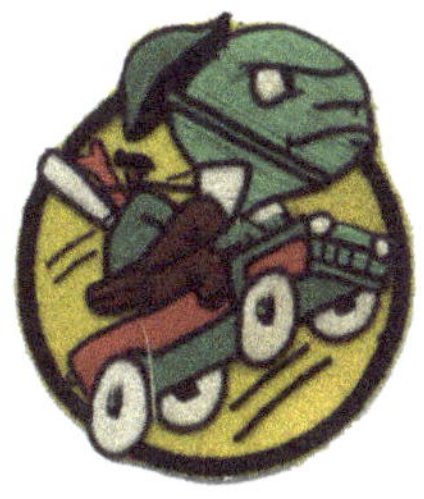
34th Combat Engineers

20th Engineer Brigade "Building Combat Power"

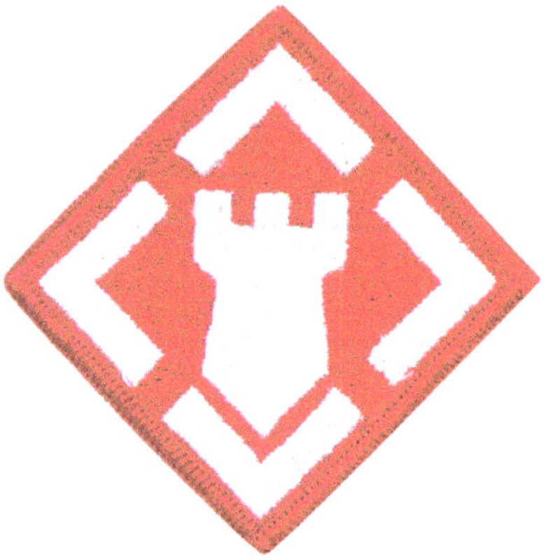

Landed in RVN: 3 Aug. 1967
Left RVN: 20 Sept. 1971
Locale: Bien Hoa

Shoulder Sleeve Insignia

A 2 $^{1}/_{4}$ inch overall square one angle up consisting of a 1 $^{1}/_{2}$ inch scarlet square bearing a white castle tower of three battlements and pointed at base paralleling the sides of the square on a 2 inch white square divided throughout by a $^{1}/_{4}$ inch wide scarlet saltire all within a $^{1}/_{8}$ inch scarlet border.

The colors scarlet and white are used for the Corps of Engineers, the castle tower being suggested by the Corps of Engineers branch insignia and its base pointed in reference to the Brigade's combat requirements. The tower also represents the Headquarters of the Brigade and the white areas, simulating carpenter squares, grouped around it allude to the engineer combat and construction groups which it serves, the four areas specifically referring to the Headquarters basic mission of command, operational planning, operational supervision, and coordination of activities. The tower and white areas also simulate heavy construction *(buildings, compounds, fortifications, bunkers, revetments, runways, roads, etc.)* and on being placed on a square allude to the establishment of bases, the red border and the red saltire referring to lines of communication. In addition, the four white areas also resemble the letter "V" for victory *(successful accomplishment)* and the Roman numeral five (V) four of which make "20," the numerical designation of the Brigade. A saltire is also the Brigade symbol used on maps.

The shoulder sleeve insignia was approved on 30 June 1967.

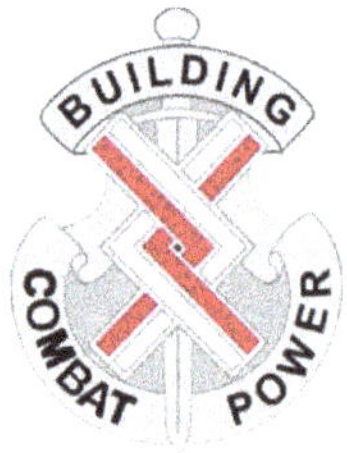
BUILDING
COMBAT
POWER

Distinctive Unit Insignia

Distinctive Unit Insignia

A silver color metal and enamel insignia 1 $^{3}/_{8}$ inches in height consisting of a silver sword point down under and over a silver encircling scroll, the upper portion surmounting the hilt and inscribed *"Building"* and the lower portion over which the blade extends inscribed *"Combat Power,"* all in black letters; overall two chevrons interlaced, apexes to the right and left and divided chevron wise white on the outside and scarlet on the inside.

The colors scarlet and white are for the Corps of Engineers. The sword and the chevrons, simulating carpenters' squares, refer to the Brigade's mission of combat and construction. The saltire, or "X" formed by the interlacing of the chevrons, denotes support and also alludes to the Brigade symbol used on Army maps.

The distinctive unit insignia was approved on 19 July 1967. One 20th Engineer soldier, Al Gore, would later become Vice President of the United States.

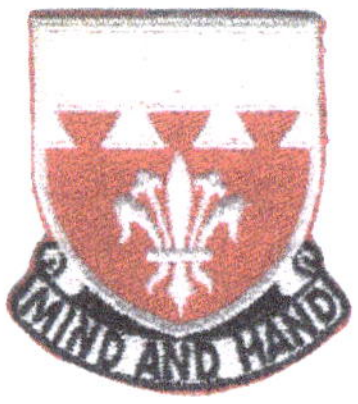
MIND AND HAND

169th Engr.Bn.

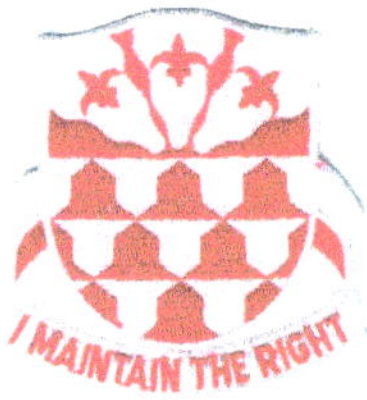
I MAINTAIN THE RIGHT

307th Abn. Engr. Bn.

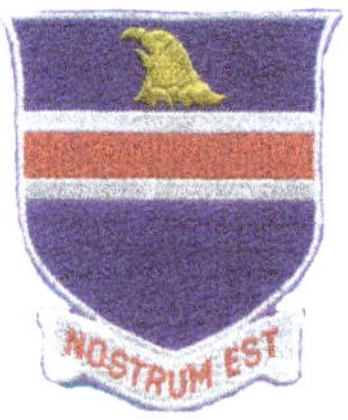
NOSTRUM EST

326th Abn.Engr. Bn.

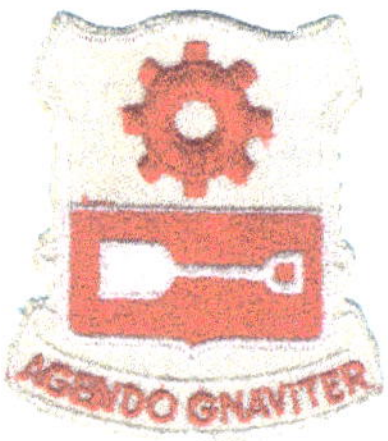
AGENDO GNAVITER

577th Engr.Bn.

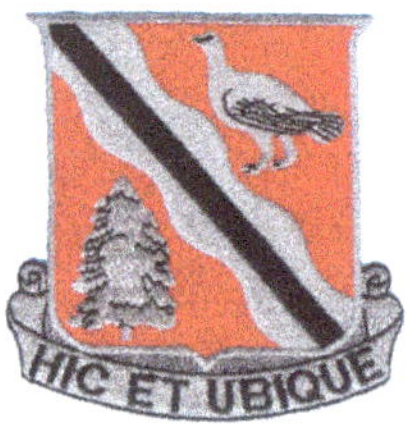
HIC ET UBIQUE

588th Engr.Bn.

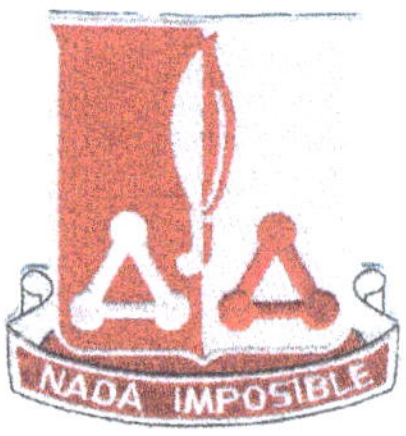
NADA IMPOSIBLE

871st Abn. Engr.Bn.

18th Military Police Brigade "Ever Vigilant"

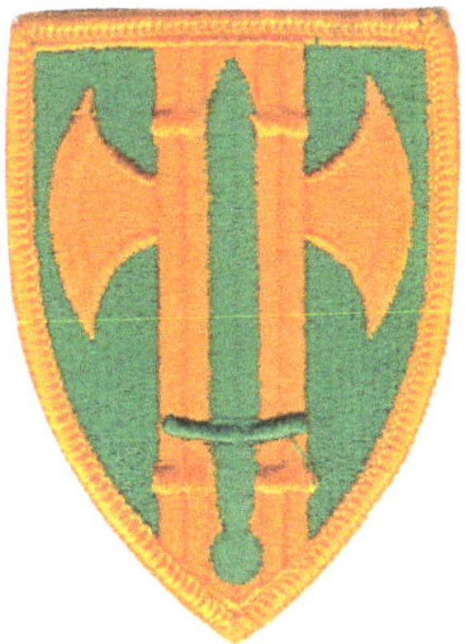

Shoulder Sleeve Insignia

A shield of $2\,{}^{1}/_{4}$ inches in width and 3 inches in height with a ${}^{1}/_{8}$ inch yellow border on a green field bearing the yellow silhouette of a Roman fasces charged with a green sword point up.

Landed in RVN: 8 Sept. 1966
Left RVN: 29 March 1973
Locale: Saigon, Long Binh

Green and yellow are the colors of the Military Police Corps. The fasces, an ancient symbol of the magistrate's authority, and the sword for the military are combined to symbolize military law and order.The shoulder sleeve insignia was approved on 1 June 1966.

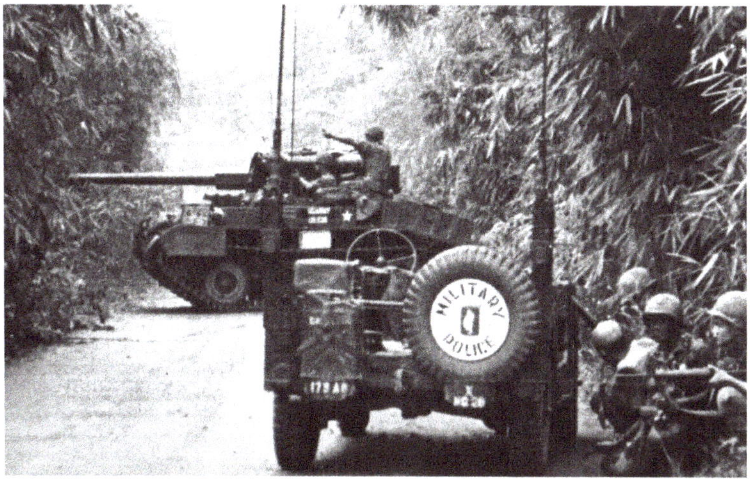
MILITARY POLICE

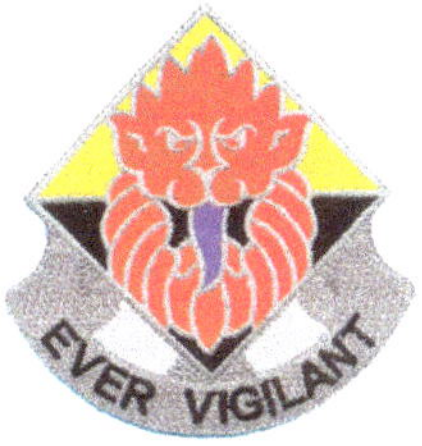
EVER VIGILANT

Distinctive Unit Insignia

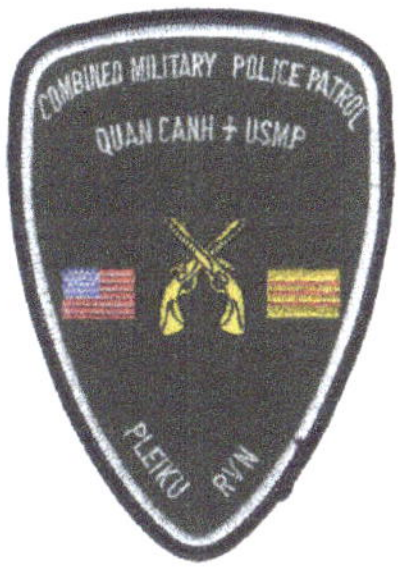
COMBINED MILITARY POLICE PATROL
QUAN CANH + USMP
PLEIKU RVN

Combined M.p. Patrol - Vietnam

Distinctive Unit Insignia

A silver color metal and enamel device $1\,{}^{1}/_{8}$ inches in height overall consisting of a square, one point up, divided horizontally, the top half yellow, the bottom half black, bearing a red lion's head guardant, mouth black and tongue blue; and attached below the square a silver scroll inscribed *"EVER VIGILANT"* in black letters.

Approved on 1 June 1966. The background represents the day *(yellow/gold color)* and the night *(black)* over which the strong watchful eye of the military police, here represented by the lion's head, is in constant vigilance.

The Brigade completed its service in Vietnam and was deactivated on 20 March 1973 in Oakland, California.

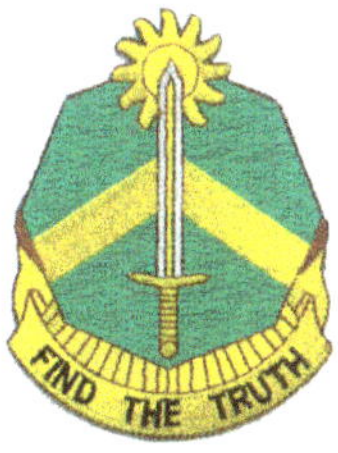
FIND THE TRUTH

8th M.P. Group

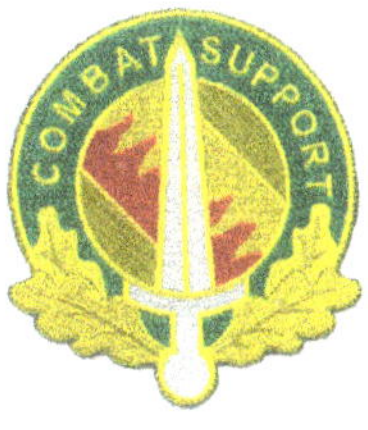
COMBAT SUPPORT

16th M.P. Group

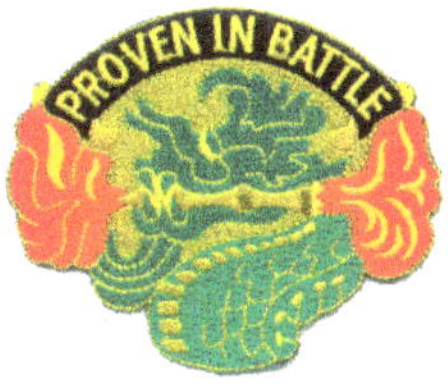
PROVEN IN BATTLE

89th M.P. Group

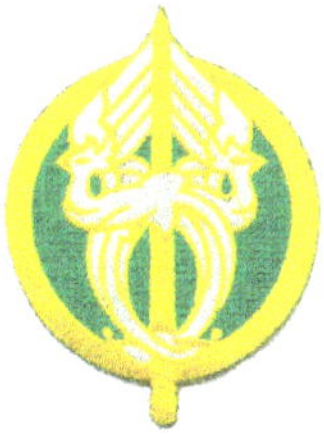

92nd M.P. Bn.

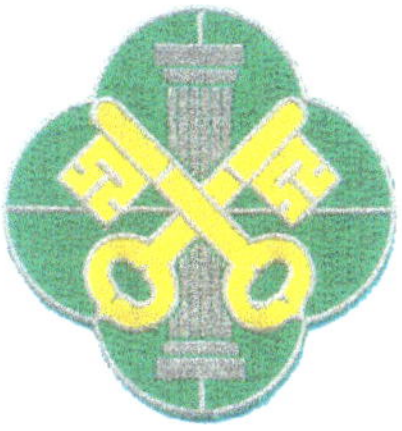

93rd M.P. Bn.

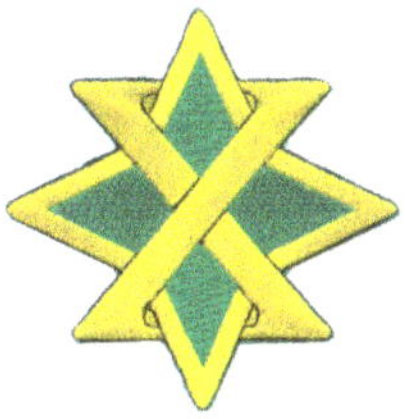

95th M.P. Bn.

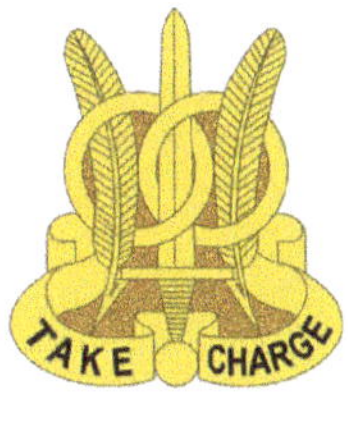
TAKE CHARGE

97th M.P. Bn.

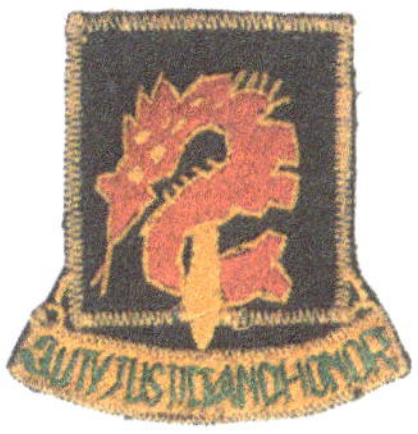

504th M.P. Bn. Vietnam

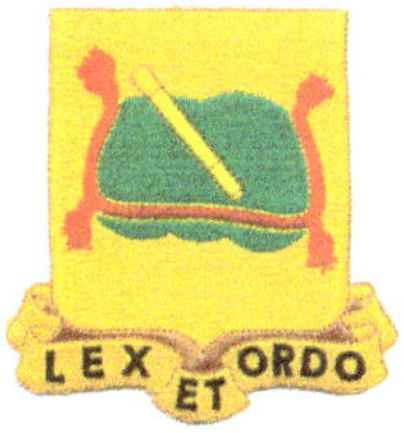
LEX ET ORDO

716th M.P. Bn.

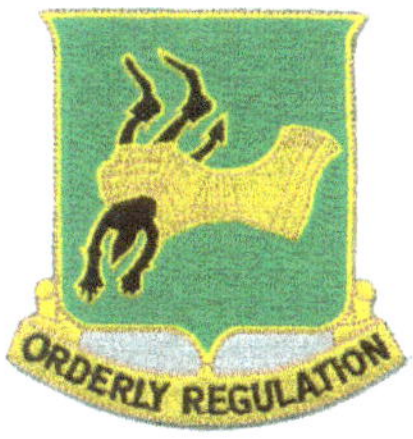
ORDERLY REGULATION

720th M.P. Bn.

1st Signal Brigade "First to Communicate"

Landed in RVN: 1 April 1966
Left RVN: 7 Nov. 1972
Locale: Long Binh

Shoulder Sleeve Insignia

On a shield 3 inches in height and 2 $\frac{1}{4}$ inches in width overall divided into three vertical stripes orange, blue and orange, the blue center stripe 1 inch in width and surmounted by an unsheathed sword, point to top, the hilt yellow and the blade forming a bolt of lightning all within a yellow $\frac{1}{8}$ inch border.

The orange field of the shield and the yellow border were suggested by the authorized shoulder sleeve insignia of the Strategic Communications Command of which the 1st Signal Brigade is a part. The lightning bolt, which also appears on the Strategic Communications Command shoulder sleeve insignia, is depicted on the distinctive insignia *(badge)* of the 1st Signal Brigade. In this instance, the lightning bolt, a symbol of communication, has been used as a sword blade and attached to a hilt, the sword thus referring to both the tactical and support mission of the organization. The blue vertical stripe with "sword" (suggested by the authorized shoulder sleeve insignia for the United States Army, Vietnam) alludes to the unit's numerical designation. The shoulder sleeve insignia was approved on 5 October 1966.

Distinctive Unit Insignia

A silver color metal and enamel device 1 1/4 inches in height overall consisting of a silver barbed arrowhead, the tip conjoined with orange flames issuing at base from each side of arrowhead, a lightning bolt superimposed in black.

The one bolt of lightning *(streak of electricity)* alludes to communications and to the numerical designation *(one)* of the organization. The barbed arrowhead with superimposed lightning bolt refers to both the tactical and strategic support mission of the organization. The flames allude to fire being the oldest source of signal communication at a distance and thus the first, the orange *"fire by night"* and the black "smoke by day."

The distinctive unit insignia was approved on 31 August 1966.

STRATCOM established the 1st Signal Brigade to exercise command and control over all Army communications-electronics resources in Southeast Asia. Scattered among 200 sites in Vietnam and Thailand, this brigade became the largest combat signal unit ever formed. One of those units *(formed in April 1969 until July that year)*, aided in the installation of modern communications equipment in Bang Phi, Thailand; improving the information networks for Southeast Asia.

Distinctive Unit Insignia

2nd Signal Group

40th Signal Bn.

125th Signal Bn.

501st Signal Bn.

39th Signal Brigade

97th Signal Bn.

369th Signal Brigade

40 Shoulder Sleeve Insignia and Crest of the U.S. Army Vietnam

U.S. Army Strategic Communications Command STRATCOM

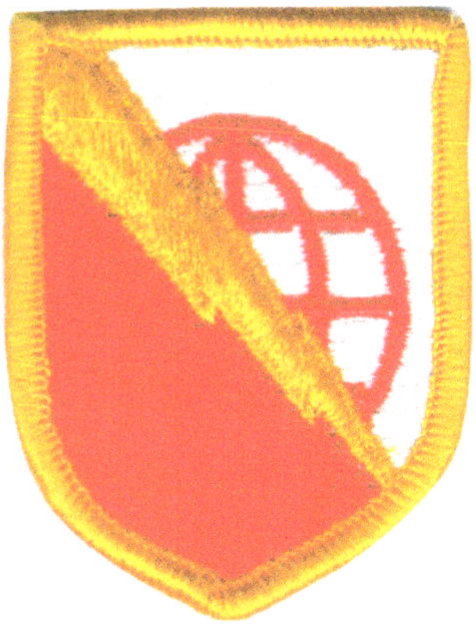

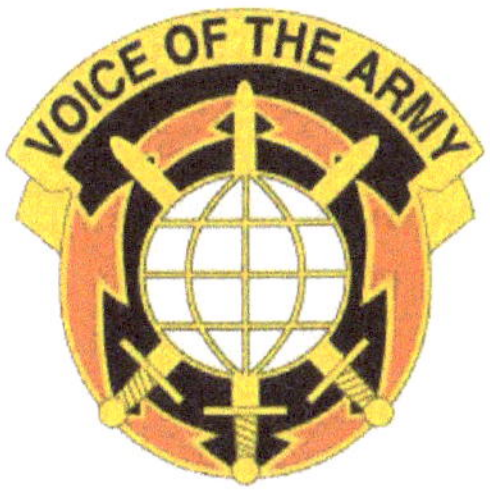
VOICE OF THE ARMY

Distinctive Unit Insignia

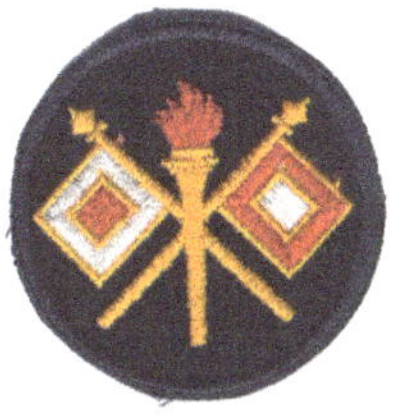

Signal Corps Logo

Shoulder Sleeve Insignia

On a shield 2 $^{1}/_{2}$ inches in height overall divided diagonally from upper left to lower right with white above and orange below, a globe with gridlines and outlines in orange above and white below and superimposed thereon from upper left to lower right a yellow lightning flash all within a $^{1}/_{8}$ inch yellow border.

The colors orange and white are representative of the Signal Corps. The globe indicates the worldwide nature of the communications controlled by the command; the lightning depicts its dynamic and strategic capabilities.

The shoulder sleeve insignia was originally approved for the U.S. Army Strategic Communications Command on 19 June 1964. It was amended to add the words *"U.S. Army"* to the designation on 31 August 1964. It was redesignated for the U.S. Army Communications Command on 18 October 1973. The insignia was redesignated for the U.S. Army Information Systems Command on 25 October 1984. It was redesignated for the U.S. Army Signal Command on 13 November 1996. It was redesignated effective 16 September 1997, for the 9th Signal Command. The insignia was redesignated effective 1 October 2002, for the U.S. Army Network Enterprise Technology Command.

Landed in RVN: 1 March 1964
Left RVN: 27 March 1973
Located: Saigon

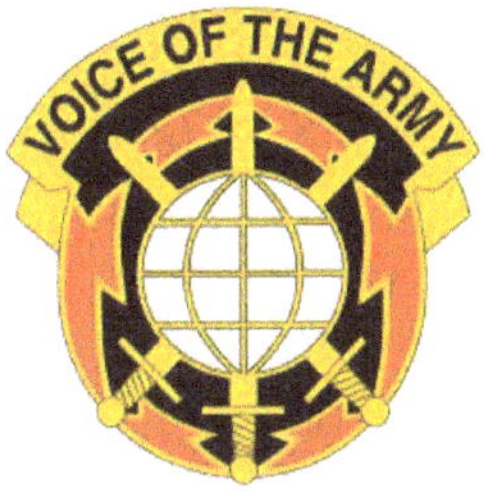
VOICE OF THE ARMY

Distinctive Unit Insignia

A gold color metal and enamel device 1 $^{1}/_{8}$ inches *(2.86 cm)* in height overall consisting of three gold swords on a black background one vertical and two saltirewise between and encircled by six orange electronic flashes and surmounted by a white globe having gold grid lines, all beneath an arched gold scroll bearing the inscription *"VOICE OF THE ARMY"* in black letters.

Orange and white are the colors representative of the Signal Corps. The swords are indicative of the military establishment supported by the Command and refer to operational readiness. The globe and electronic flashes, adapted from the shoulder sleeve insignia, symbolize the worldwide aspects of communications and the organization's dynamic and strategic capabilities.

The distinctive unit insignia was originally approved for the U.S. Army Strategic Communications Command on 27 February 1969. It was redesignated for the U.S. Army Communications Command on 18 October 1973. The insignia was redesignated for the U.S. Army Information Systems Command on 25 October 1984. It was redesignated for the U.S. Army Signal Command on 13 November 1996. It was redesignated effective 16 September 1997, for the 9th Signal Command. The insignia was redesignated effective 1 October 2002, for the U.S. Army Network Enterprise Technology Command.

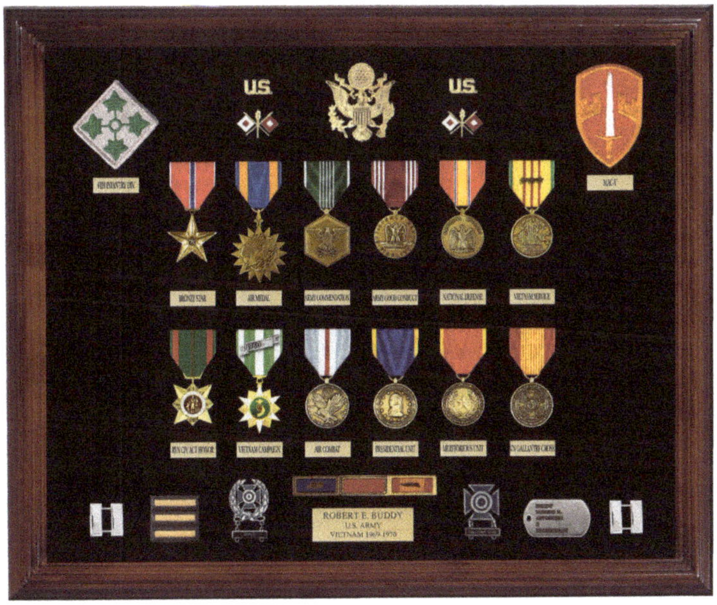

44th Medical Brigade "Dragon Medics"

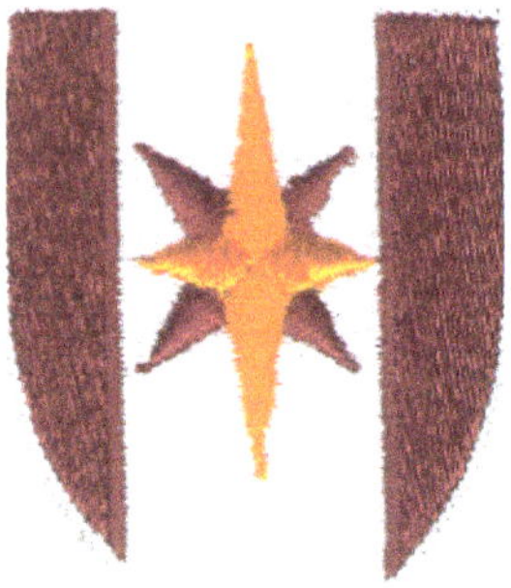

Landed in RVN: 24 April 1966
Left RVN: 14 Dec. 1970
Locale: Long Binh

Shoulder Sleeve Insignia

On a white shield within a 1/8 inch white border, 2 1/2 inches in height and 2 inches in width overall, a four-pointed gold star with longer vertical points is superimposed on a maroon four pointed star all of equal length between two maroon flanks.

Maroon and white are the colors used for the Army Medical Service. The gold star superimposed over the maroon star is symbolic of the unit's mission of command and control over medical units. The four points of each taken together allude to the organization's numerical designation.

The shoulder sleeve insignia was originally approved for the 44th Medical Brigade on 5 October 1966. It was redesignated for the 44th Medical Command effective 16 October 2001. The insignia was redesignated for the 44th Medical Brigade with the description updated effective 16 April 2010.

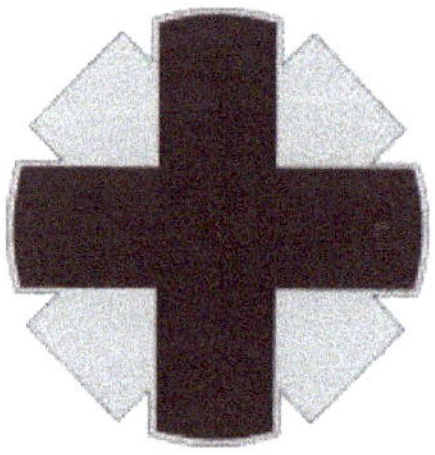

Distinctive Unit Insignia

Distinctive Unit Insignia

A silver color metal and enamel device 1 1/8 inches in diameter consisting of a silver saltire (cross), the four arms equal and with straight ends, surmounted by a maroon cross, the four arms equal and with arched ends.

Maroon and white *(silver)* are the colors used for the Army Medical Service and the two crosses refer to the medical and surgical mission of the organization while the four arms of each cross taken together allude to the organization's numerical designation. The distinctive unit insignia was originally approved for the 44th Medical Brigade on 12 August 1966.

US Army Medical Command, Vietnam

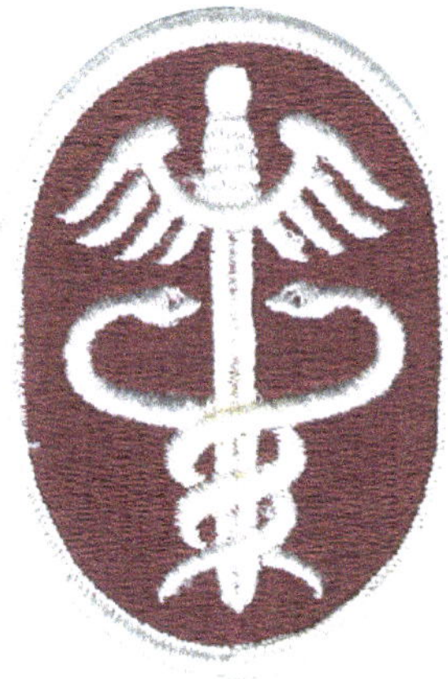

Landed in RVN: 1 March 1970
Left RVN: 30 April 1972
Locale: South Vietnam

Shoulder Sleeve Insignia

On a maroon oval 2 1/4 inches in width and 3 inches in height overall, a sword with hilt at the top and hand guard in the form of a pair of stylized wings, and below two serpents with heads facing center and bodies entwined about the blade all in white and all within an 1/8 inch white border.

Maroon and white are the colors used for the Army Medical Department. The wings and serpents allude to the caduceus symbol representing all medical services and the sword in place of the staff relates to the United States Army. The sword with point to base is symbolic of sacrifice and mercy and alludes to the noncombatant role of the medical services.

The insignia was redesignated for US Army Medical Command effective 2 October 1994, with the description revised.

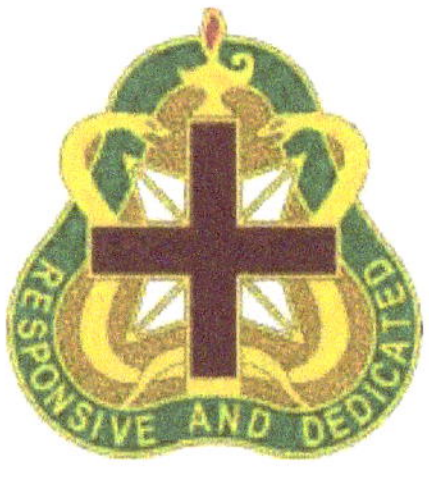
RESPONSIVE AND DEDICATED

Distinctive Unit Insignia

Distinctive Unit Insignia

A gold color metal and enamel device 1 1/4 inches in height overall consisting of a green pear-shaped scroll bearing in gold letters on the lower half the words *"RESPONSIVE AND DEDICATED"* and containing a maroon Greek cross surmounted by a gold lamp enflamed red and issuant out of each of the four angles a white pointed ray enclosed at either side by a gold serpent with heads at top facing inward and tails entwined behind the center of the cross and curving down at either side.

Maroon and white are the colors used for the Army Medical Department. Green was the color first used in the medieval age for academic gowns for medicine and is currently the academic color for medicine. In 1847, green was prescribed as the first Army Medical Department color.

1st Logistical Command "1st Log"

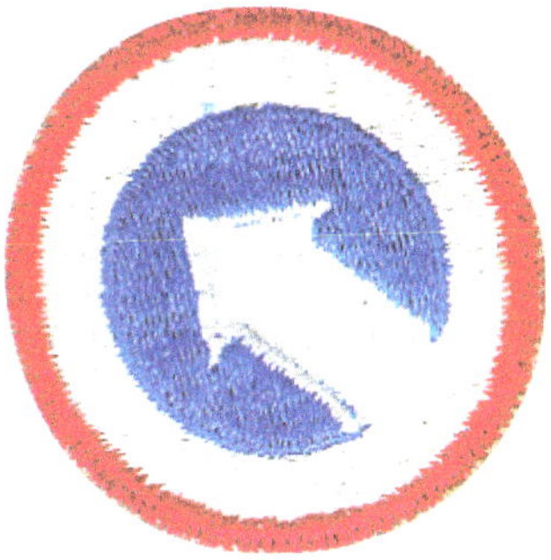

Shoulder Sleeve Insignia

On a disc 2 inches in diameter overall, between a blue center and a $^{1}/_{8}$ inch red border, a $^{9}/_{32}$ inch white band. Issuing from the white band on a 45° diagonal from lower right to upper left, a white arrow, the arrowhead terminating above the center of the blue disc. The insignia was originally approved for the 1st Logistical Command on 15 May 1952. It was amended to change the description on 23 January 1968. On 18 February 1971, the insignia was redesignated for the Headquarters and Headquarters Company and Special Troops, 1st Field Army Support Command. The insignia was redesignated for the 1st Field Army Support Command on 4 June 1971. It was redesignated for the 1st Corps Support Command on 8 September 1972. It was redesignated for the 1st Support Command on 22 October 1980. The insignia was redesignated for the 1st Sustainment Command with the description updated on 6 April 2006.

Landed in RVN: 30 March 1965
Left RVN: 7 Dec. 1970
Locale: Long Binh

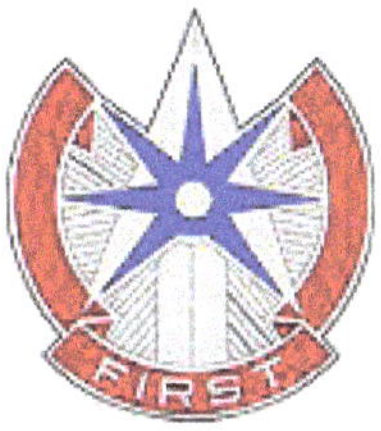
FIRST

Distinctive Unit Insignia

Distinctive Unit Insignia

A silver color metal and enamel device 1 $^{1}/_{4}$ inches *(3.18 cm)* in height overall consisting of a silver arrow issuing in pale charged with a blue mullet of seven points surmounted by a plate, all within a red scroll inscribed in base *"FIRST"* in silver letters.

The arrow alludes to speed and effectiveness in fulfilling the mission of the organization. It also represents combat capability. The seven-pointed mullet is indicative of the seven continents of the world and refers to the ability of the Command to serve in all areas.

The insignia was originally approved for the 1st Logistical Command on 19 April 1968. It was redesignated for the Headquarters and Headquarters Company and Special Troops, 1st Field Army Support Command and amended to change the symbolism of the design on 18 February 1971. The insignia was redesignated for the 1st Field Army Support Command on 4 June 1971. On 8 September 1972, it was redesignated for the 1st Corps Support Command. The insignia was approved for the 1st Support Command on 22 October 1980. It was redesignated for the 1st Sustainment Command with the description updated on 6 April 2006.

Some Other Key Transportation Units

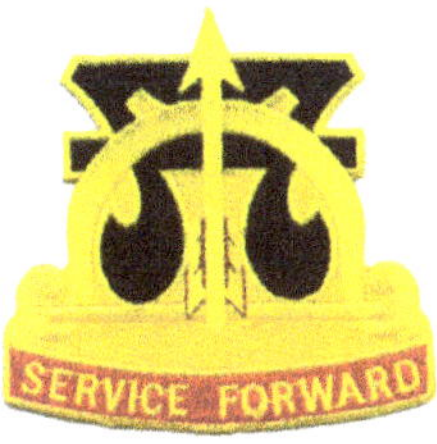
SERVICE FORWARD

48th Transp.Group

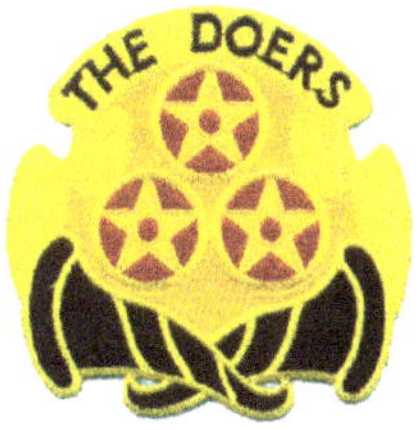
THE DOERS

6th Transp. Bn.

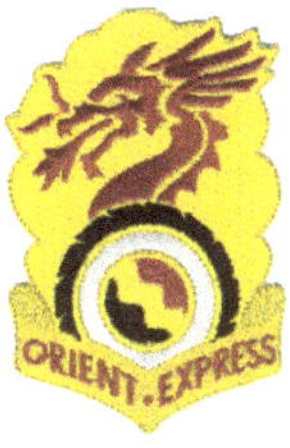
ORIENT EXPRESS

7th Transp. Bn.

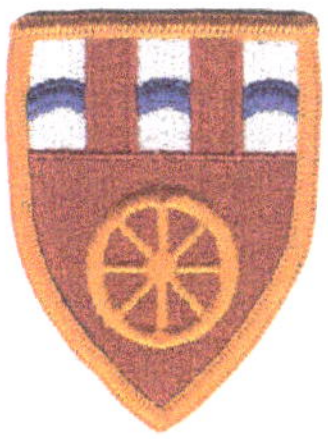

11th Transp. Bn.

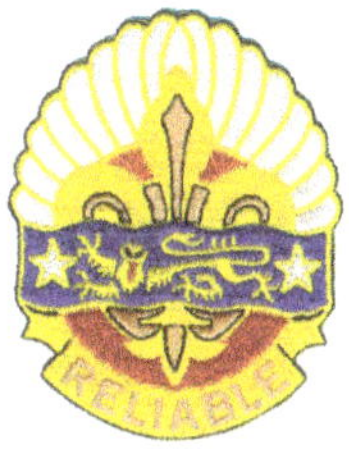
RELIABLE

14th Transp. Bn.

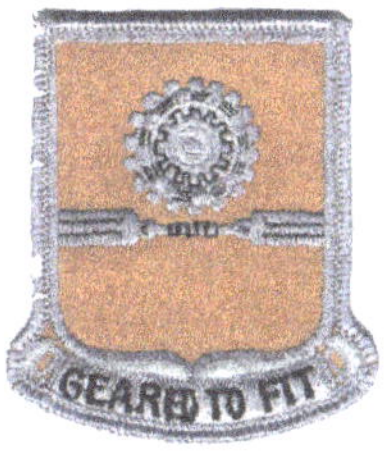
GEARED TO FIT

27th Transp Bn.

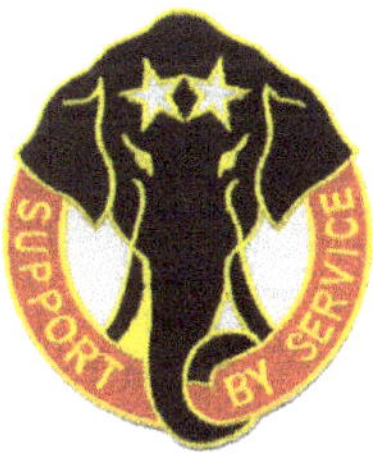
SUPPORT BY SERVICE

36th Transp. Bn.

15th Support Brigade "Wagonmaster Brigade"

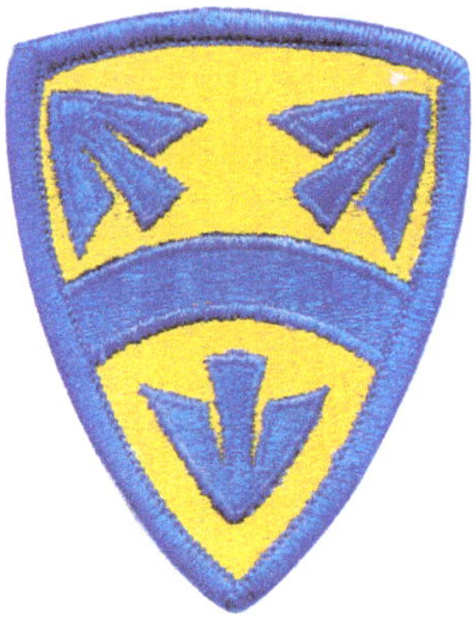

Shoulder Sleeve Insignia

The 15th Support Brigade shoulder sleeve insignia was approved on 20 December 1966 for the unit that had been constituted the previous May and activated 1 July 1966 at Fort Hood.

The 15th Support Brigade unit patch is designed like a shield, with a horizontal arch in the center to represent the vital support the organization provided units. Broad arrows flowing out from the arch denote action and, combined with the arch, visually express the Briagde's motto of *"Support The Action."* The trio of arrowheads also stand for three essential support functions the Brigade provided: Supply, Maintenance, and Services. Additionally, the head of an arrow simulates the Roman *"V"* for five, with three fives indicating the Brigade's numerical designation.

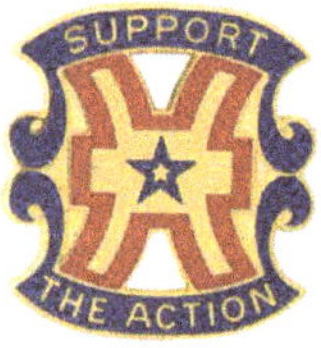
SUPPORT
THE ACTION

Distinctive Unit Insignia

Landed in RVN: 29 Nov. 1966
Left RVN: 20 Oct. 1967
inactivated
Locale: Long Binh, Chu Lai

Distinctive Unit Insignia

A gold, red and blue color metal and enamel device 1 $^1/_8$ inches *(2.86 cm)* in height overall consisting of a red multi lane highway bearing a blue outline star, all surmounting with blue scrolls lined gold arched with the inscription *"SUPPORT"* and across the base *"THE ACTION"* in gold letters.

Red, white and blue are our National colors. The star is indicative of superior administrative and logistical support.

The 15th Support Brigade was inactivated in Vietnam and its assets were used to form the the 23rd Infantry "Americal" Division Support Command in December 1967.

4th Transportation Command

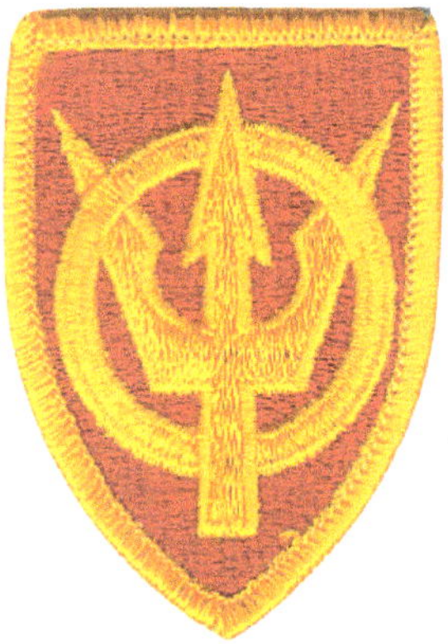

Shoulder Sleeve Insignia

On a brick red shield 2 inches in width and 2 inches in height overall and within a $^1/_8$ inch yellow border a yellow annulet and trident interlaced.

Brick red and yellow are the colors used for Transportation. The wheel, a symbol for movement and the trident, an attribute of Poseidon *(God of the Sea in Greek mythology)* allude to the mission of the organization in the movement of vital cargo across land and waterways.

The shoulder sleeve insignia was originally approved for the 4th Transportation Command on 28 June 1967. It was redesignated for the 4th Transportation Brigade on 13 May 1975. The insignia was redesignated effective 16 February 1981, for the 4th Transportation Command.

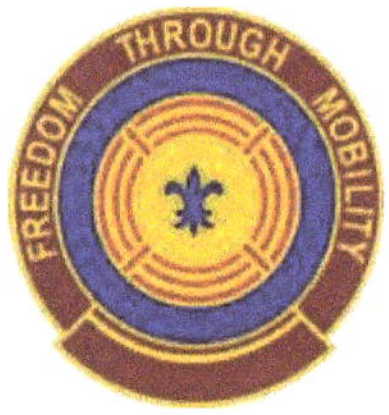
FREEDOM THROUGH MOBILITY

Distinctive Unit Insignia

Landed in RVN: 8 Aug. 1965
Left RVN: 26 June 1972
Locale: Saigon

Distinctive Unit Insignia

A gold color metal and enamel device 1 $^3/_{16}$ inches in height overall consisting of three concentric red *(scarlet)* circles bound with four gold bands saltire wise and bearing at center a yellow disc charged with a blue fleur-de-lis and all encircled by a blue border within a continuous brick red scroll inscribed *"FREEDOM THROUGH MOBILITY"* in gold letters. Brick red and golden yellow are the colors used for Transportation. The organization's mission in France as a Port Headquarters and Headquarters Company during World War II is symbolized by the fleur-de-lis and the circular blue band alluding to a Port of Embarkation or terminal. The three scarlet concentric bands refer to the three Meritorious Unit Commendations-two for France and one for Vietnam, awarded to the organization.

5th Transportation Command

No Distinctive Unit Insignia Authorized

Shoulder Sleeve Insignia

A round bottom shield 2 inches in width and 2 $\frac{1}{2}$ inches in height having within a $\frac{1}{8}$ inch yellow border upon a field of brick red a yellow wedge extending from top to bottom with a yellow disc centered on and over it, that portion of the disc on the wedge in brick red and charged in center with a yellow five-pointed star. Yellow and brick red are the colors traditionally associated with the Transportation Corps. The wedge or V-shape indicates the numerical designation of the Command. The disc represents the wheel, a symbol basic to transportation and the star at its hub represents the command function. The shoulder sleeve insignia was approved on 6 April 1967.

Landed in RVN: 1 Oct. 1966
Left RVN: 13 June 1972
Located in Qui Nhon, Da Nang

124th Transportation Command

Landed in RVN: 1 Oct. 1966
Left RVN: 1 May 1972
Locale: Cam Ranh Bay

Shoulder Sleeve Insignia

On a brick red shield 2 inches in width overall a yellow wheel between two wings, all within a $\frac{1}{8}$ inch yellow border.

Brick red and yellow are the colors used for Transportation. The winged wheel symbolizes two of the roles of Transportation : air and rail movement. The shoulder sleeve insignia was approved on 1 June 1967.

The 124th was responsible for operation of the Port of Cam Ranh Bay.

No Distinctive Unit Insignia Authorized

125th Transportation Command

Landed in RVN: 4 Oct. 1966
Left RVN: 14 Feb. 1970
Locale: Ton Son Nhut

Shoulder Sleeve Insignia

An upright rectangle 2 inches in width and 3 inches in height arched at base and having within a $\frac{1}{8}$ inch yellow border a brick red field charged with a blue anchor surmounted with a yellow wheel.

Brick red and yellow are the colors used for Transportation. The wheel symbolizes the basic aspects of movement and with the anchor refers to the organization's mission in support of amphibious operations. The shoulder sleeve insignia was approved on 7 June 1967.

No Distinctive Unit Insignia auuthorized

Combat Developments Command

VISION TO VICTORY

Distinctive Unit Insignia

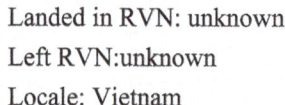

Shoulder Sleeve Insignia

On a red disk 2 inches in diameter a white arrowhead, point up, containing a blue five-pointed star, its upper point extended.

The star is symbolic of command and its extended upper point emphasizes direction and purpose. The arrowhead denotes the combat aspect of the operation.

The shoulder sleeve insignia was approved for the U.S. Army Combat Developments Command on 9 July 1962. It was amended to specifically authorized wear for the Office, Commanding General, United States Army Combat Developments Command and subordinate elements on 23 July 1963. The insignia was cancelled on 12 July 1973.

Landed in RVN: unknown
Left RVN:unknown
Locale: Vietnam

Distinctive Unit Insignia

A device of silver color metal and enamel 1 ¼ inches in height overall consisting of a red arrowhead with point up bearing three silver stars in a triangle, the arrowhead trailing five pointed silver rays; passing in front of the rays from either side of the arrowhead an elliptical blue scroll inscribed with the words *"VISION TO VICTORY"* in silver letters.

The red arrowhead, pointing up, is symbolic of the Command's mission to produce improvements in the Army in the field through an upward looking, aggressive Combat Developments program. The rays, reading from right to left, emphasize the five functions of land combat: Fire; Movement; Control *(including Command and Communication)*; Intelligence; and Support *(including both Combat Support and Combat Service Support)*; and symbolize the dynamic relationship which exists between these functions. The stars represent the threefold mission of the Command in determining "How the Army will fight," *"How the Army will be equipped,"* and "How the Army will be organized." The unit's motto, *"Vision To Victory,"* expresses the spirit and motivation of the organization.

The distinctive unit insignia was originally approved for the noncolor bearing units of the U.S. Army Combat Developments Command. It was redesignated for the U.S. Army Combat Developments Experimentation Command on 6 August 1973.

ARMY COMMENDATION
ARMY GOOD CONDUCT
NATIONAL DEFENSE
VIETNAM SERVICE
1960
VIETNAM CAMPAIGN
MERITORIOUS UNIT
VN GALLANTRY CROSS
VIETNAM DEFENSE
CHARLES H. MOORE
1ST BATTALION, 7TH CAVALRY
1ST CAVALRY DIVISION
REPUBLIC OF VIETNAM 1969

U.S. Army Materiel Command (AMC)

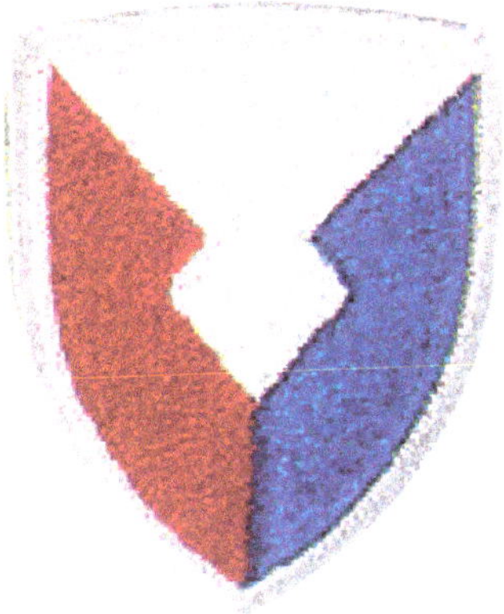

Landed in RVN: 1965
Left RVN: 1971
Locale: Vietnam

Shoulder Sleeve Insignia

On a shield $2\,{}^{1}/_{2}$ inches overall in height divided per pairle *(three sections)* white, red and blue, a white lozenge in fess (center) point all within a ${}^{1}/_{8}$ inch white border.

The lozenge and white areas represent the command and control elements of the organization with the red area used to represent the Army and the blue area industry. The white area also alludes to the flow of materiel through the equal and combined efforts of the Army and industry as directed.

The insignia was originally approved for US Army Materiel Command on 29 Oct. 1962; redesignated for US Army Development and Readiness Command *(DARCOM)* on 23 Feb 1976; and redesignated for US Army Materiel Command on 23 Nov 1984.

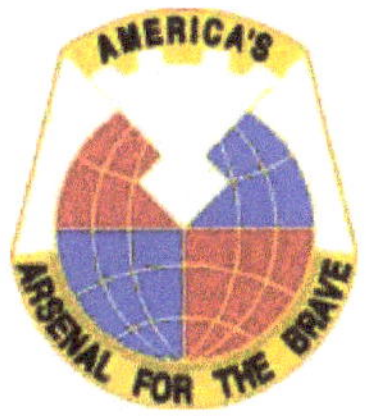
AMERICA'S
ARSENAL FOR THE BRAVE

Distinctive Unit Insignia

Distinctive Unit Insignia

A gold color metal and enamel device $1\,{}^{3}/_{16}$ inches in height overall consisting of a globe quarterly scarlet and ultramarine blue gridlined gold surmounting the base of a white truncated pyramid; arcing between and above the pyramid a gold motto scroll inscribed *"AMERICA'S"* in black letters and arcing below the globe a gold motto scroll inscribed *"ARSENAL FOR THE BRAVE"* in black letters. Overall issuing from the center of the globe to the upper scroll a white notched pile arched and embattled of four merlons.

Elements of the insignia design were adapted from the authorized shoulder sleeve insignia and mission of the United States Army Materiel Command. The white crenellated design at the top of the insignia refers to command and control. The four merlons, which simulate the cogs in a gear wheel, allude to the four major functions of the command's mission.

The pyramid, a symbol of strength and support, is truncated to indicate the continuing research, development, production, procurement, storage, transportation, standardization and distribution of materiel as assigned or required. The white areas simulate the letter *"M"* for materiel and the globe indicates the world wide scope of the Command's responsibility in providing technical and professional guidance and assistance for planning and conducting logistics services of the Army elements of unified and specified commands and other United States and foreign customers, with scarlet referring to the military and blue referring to industry.

The command's motto, *"AMERICA's ARSENAL FOR THE BRAVE"* reflects the mission of providing outstanding support to the total Army.

The distinctive unit insignia was originally approved Army Materiel Command on 2 June 1969; redesignated for Material Development and Readiness Command *(DARCOM)* on 23 Feb. 1976; and redesignated for Army Material Command on 23 Nov. 1984. It was cancelled on 24 Dec. 1992 with the current design and motto change approved on 24 Dec. 1992.

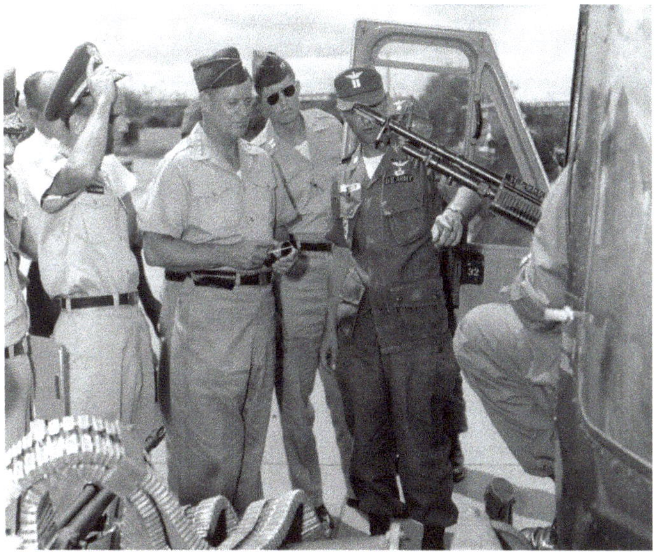

Military Traffic Management and Terminal Service

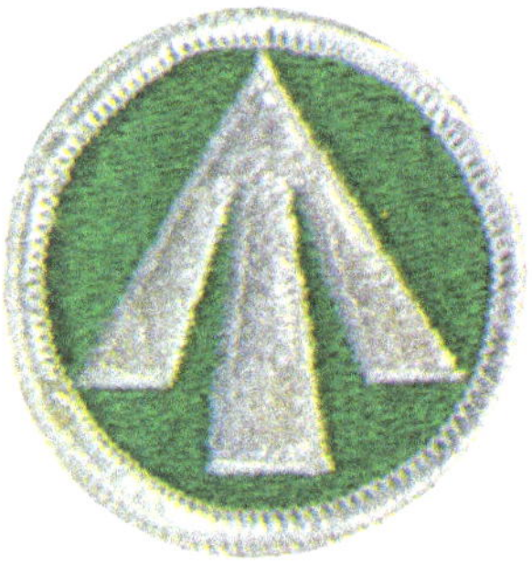

Landed in RVN: 24 June 1965
Left RVN: 1971?
Locale: Saigon

Shoulder Sleeve Insignia

On a green disc with a 1/8 inch white border 2 inches in diameter overall, a white broad arrow, point up.

The green disc represents the "Go" signal used for traffic control of land transport. It is symbolic of the Command's *"Can Do", "Go"* attitude in the control of traffic, land transportation and common-user ocean terminal service. The arrow alludes to the military auspices of the organization and to the speed with which it accomplishes its mission. The three prongs represent the three military departments of the Department of Defense and the joint aspects of its responsibilities and manning.

The shoulder sleeve insignia was originally approved for the Military Traffic Management and Terminal Service on 17 August 1965. It was redesignated for the Military Traffic Management Command on 10 December 1974. The insignia was redesignated effective 1 January 2004, for the Military Surface Deployment and Distribution Command, with the description updated.

Distinctive Unit Insignia

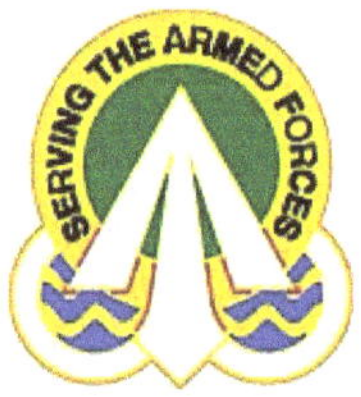
SERVING THE ARMED FORCES

Distinctive Unit Insignia

A gold color metal and enamel device 1 3/16 inches *(3.02 cm)* in height consisting of two discs within two white annulets conjoined horizontally, each disc composed of six horizontal way bands, alternately gold and blue, the upper sections surmounted by a larger green disc within a gold annulet the upper part inscribed *"SERVING THE ARMED FORCES"* in black letters; overall a white broad arrow, the point terminating on the green disc and the base extending beyond the white annulets.

The green disc, representing the land, bridges the smaller wavy disc, representing the oceans; they refer to land transportation and ocean terminal service.

The three annulets simulating wheels allude to motion. The white broad arrow over the discs provides direction; it stands for control of the movement of cargo and passengers, i.e., traffic management.

The arrowhead and the colors green and white are taken from the shoulder sleeve insignia of the Command to indicate that the units are components of that organization; the green is symbolic of the Command's *"Can Do", "Go"* attitude in the exercise of its traffic management, land transportation and terminal service responsibilities; the arrow also alludes to the military auspices of the organization, the speed with which it accomplishes its mission and the air transport functions which it performs.

The distinctive unit insignia was originally approved for the Military Traffic Management and Terminal Service on 6 January 1969. It was redesignated for the Military Traffic Management Command on 10 December 1974. The insignia was redesignated effective 1 January 2004, for the Military Surface Deployment and Distribution Command, with the description updated and the symbolism revised.

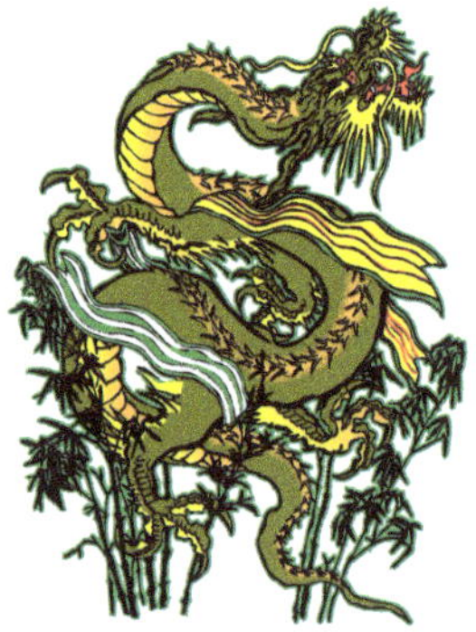

www.ingramcontent.com/pod-product-compliance
Lightning Source LLC
Chambersburg PA
CBHW051321110526
44590CB00031B/4423